Trials, Errors
and
Misdemeanours

by

Margaret Barnes.

Published by Scribbling Advocate in 2019

ISBN 978-1-9164471-5-8

Cover Design by
BerniStevensdesign.com
Depicting Cloisters Middle Temple

Foreword

I spent my working life as an advocate in the Criminal Justice System of England and Wales, first as a solicitor and then as a barrister. I was lucky enough to practice at the Bar when legal aid was more readily available. Those of us who worked at the Criminal Bar were called 'the worthies' because of the disparity between our incomes and those of barristers who did civil work, but one could earn a decent living.

These tales and anecdotes are my experiences told without elaboration. I have changed the names to protect both the innocent and the guilty but the events they describe are true.

They took place in a variety of courts up and down the country. I have not attempted to describe them. Some, like the Assize Court at Lancaster and No 1 Court at the Central Criminal Court, are huge impressive rooms where the presiding judge looks down on the barristers, clerks and police officers. Most are more modest.

Our criminal justice system is under threat as every aspect of it is starved of funds. A trial to decide the guilt or innocence of the citizen depends on all those involved, the police as investigators, the prosecuting authorities, solicitors and barristers playing their part effectively. Lawyers traditionally say little about the role they play in ensuring justice for both victims and defendants. I hope this memoir will improve understanding of the delicate balance that ensures a fair trial; that the guilty are convicted and the innocent go free. Anything else undermines our society and our belief in the rule of law.

This book is dedicated to all those advocates who fight for their client without fear or favour, and in particular to Kate Mallinson who throughout her life did just that.

Turning Point

I didn't see the significance of one chance meeting. I thought it was just another turn in the road, a way through the latest problem, not something that would change the course of my life. I was in a hard place; a difficult tutorial with a lecturer in the biochemistry department at Sheffield University had ended when I confessed I hated the course, and was sure I would not pass the exams at the end of the second year.

Despite his reassurances, I knew I did not want to carry on into the third year. At best I would only scrape through my finals, and then what sort of future did I have? I didn't want to teach and the suggestion I could become a forensic scientist left me cold. I was struggling as it was, bursting into tears when the strain of the work in the laboratory got too much for me. But going home and facing my parents, who were so proud of me, was unbearable. The thought of my father's face, trying to hide his distress, his pale blue eyes struggling with tears as he tried to tell me that he simply wanted me to be happy. And my mother would be cross; the sacrifices they had both made so I could go to university would have been pointless.

I left my tutor's room feeling sick as I wrestled with the problem of my future; the smell of formaldehyde wafting from the laboratories didn't help. I forced myself to put one foot in front of the other, along the corridor and through the double doors with the Krebs cycle etched in the glass above. I heard, as if somewhere far away, the sounds of chattering voices and the clack of my heels on the black-and-white tiled floor of the entrance hall.

I walked along the path towards the Students' Union, my mind whirling as I went through the alternative roads I might travel. I crossed Western Bank, hardly noticing the traffic until a car hooted at me. Once on the far pavement I turned to cross the lawns towards the door to the Union. I was so distracted that I jumped when a voice said to me, 'You look like you're rather upset. Can I help?'

In front of me was the stocky figure of the Dean of the Law Faculty, Professor Wood. I knew him because I had stood for and been elected to the Students' Representative Council and the law professor was the Staff Treasurer.

He smiled, encouraging me to tell him what was troubling me. I swallowed hard and then, like a pipe bursting, the whole story came out: how unhappy I was, how I hated the long days in the labs; how awful the prospect of failing and how upset my parents would be.

'Come and see me on Monday afternoon and I'll see what I can do. I think I can find you a place in the Law Faculty.'

The Articled Clerk

After obtaining a very creditable upper second at the University of Sheffield I was lucky enough to obtain articles, as they were then called, with a large firm of solicitors who had a number of offices in and around Blackpool, Lancashire. I was articled to the local MP, later to become Sir Walter Clegg. He spent most of his time at the Palace of Westminster so I worked with another solicitor in the Fleetwood office.

Initially I was taught how to do conveyancing – that rather arcane procedure by which the ownership of land is transferred from one person to another. Today most land is registered and the transaction is mainly conducted online, but then there were mountains of paperwork going back and forth between the solicitors acting for the vendor and those for the purchaser. Even this rather routine work had its moments. Completion of the transaction took place at the office of the vendor's solicitors. I visited most of the other solicitors' premises in Fleetwood and the surrounding area.

One firm worked in the sort of offices that would have seemed familiar to Dickens. Not a female in sight and the male clerks working at stand-up writing slopes. Another completion took me up to Ambleside to the firm of William Heelis – Beatrix Potter's husband. I suspect very little had changed since his death. As I completed the transaction, checking the copies of documents against the original and handing over a draft for the purchase price, a golden cocker spaniel snored under the desk.

My worst moment was when I went to a firm in Lancaster who were the land agents for the Duke of Devonshire. The documents of the Duke's land holdings were in large blue leather-bound books. The solicitor took one down from the twenty or thirty ranged on bookshelves that lined the walls. He opened it at what appeared to be the relevant page – my client was purchasing a piece of farmland from the estate, which was identified by its field number. I searched the map I had been shown but couldn't find the number I was looking for. After a few minutes the solicitor asked me what was wrong. When I explained he too looked at the maps. Eventually he said he thought we had the wrong part of the estate, took down another of the large tomes and after a brief search found the correct parcel of land.

As I became more experienced I did other work, including establishing the company that manufactures 'Fisherman's Friends' cough lozenges. But more exciting was when

I was sent to court to sit behind counsel. My
path to becoming a barrister had begun.

Fishing and Fishermen

Fleetwood was a fishing port when I began my articles. Life was hard; the men left the port in small fishing boats sometimes for three weeks at a time. Once back on land and with money in their pockets they drank their way round the town. There were fights most weekends and people got hurt. One young fisherman ended up at Preston Crown Court facing a charge of assault occasioning grievous bodily harm. He pleaded guilty. The tariff for the offence, usually referred to as GBH, was an immediate prison sentence. In mitigation, counsel called the skipper of the boat on which he sailed. The ship's captain described the defendant's working conditions, which he said were worse than any prison. His work took him to Icelandic waters where he had to climb the rigging and chip the ice off it to prevent the boat capsizing. The judge, who was a local man, exercised his discretion and accepted that the defendant was an industrious young man whose life was hard and gave him a suspended sentence. That seemed a just ruling.

I wasn't always so impressed. There was a County Court judge who told one client who was seeking a divorce on the grounds of her husband's cruelty that she shouldn't have waited up for him when he went out drinking. Or the magistrates who asked a woman who was complaining of being assaulted by her husband if her father had been a fisherman. She told them he had. 'And your grandfather?' She confirmed he too had been at sea. 'And did your father hit your mother when he came back from the pub having been at sea for three weeks?'

'Yes,' she said, 'he did.'

'So you knew what would happen when you got married, didn't you?' They weren't expecting an answer and dismissed her application for a separation order.

I took instructions from a number of women who had been violently attacked by their fisherman husbands but none so badly as the young woman who was seven months pregnant and whose husband had punched her repeatedly over all her body. She said she had done her best to protect her unborn child. She was admitted to hospital and nearly lost her baby. When she came to see me to obtain an injunction against him her face still bore the bruises from his vicious assault. That was bad enough, but when the child was born he was deaf, probably the result of the battering the poor woman had endured.

She did divorce him, but so many women put up with violence from their husbands because of the financial difficulties they would face as lone parents. It was less acceptable then, and few of them could earn a living on their own. Divorce was a luxury they couldn't afford.

A Boundary Dispute

Articled clerks always got the worst jobs. On my first day in the office amongst the files I was given was one very thick bundle of papers. It contained correspondence going back for about six years. Our clients owned a bungalow on the main road east out of Cleveleys. The land had originally been farmland but strip development had taken place. The farmer who had sold off the plots of land had retained a strip wide enough for his farm machinery to get into his fields. But that had been many years before, and his tractor was now too wide to get along the track. He maintained the owners of the bungalows on each side had planted hedges on his land, which had matured and were now impeding his access.

Our clients disputed this and argued that the hedges were inside the boundaries. Among the papers were copies of the plans from their conveyance. Land in north Lancashire was not registered at the time. I looked carefully at the plans but they were of very little assistance. They were endorsed with the classic and meaningless phrase: 'This plan is for the purposes of identification only and not of delineation.' That meant they were not to scale and, anyway, the thick red pencil line would have made it difficult to measure with any accuracy.

I dreaded telephone calls from our clients, which were made slightly worse because the wife's voice sounded like that of a tenor and I couldn't tell which of them I was speaking too. Fortunately the solicitor for the farmer thought the whole thing was hilarious and, in his view, incapable of solution.

'My client will just bulldoze his way through. They'll want to sue for the damage to their hedge and you'll tell them that is not a good idea. Then it will all die down until the next time. Just put the file to the bottom of the pile and tell them you're working on it.'

I wasn't too happy with that. I wanted to make a good impression with my principal and with the clients. However, I thought the farmer's solicitor was probably right so I took his advice. My salvation came in the form of Trevor, a rather chubby young man who was the new articled clerk.

He had already been given a few files to work on when he came into my room to see if I needed any help.

'Well, there is this,' I said, handing him the dog-eared bundle.

A couple of weeks later he came into the office looking very smug. 'I've solved that boundary dispute,' he said. 'I went round, got the farmer there, together with our clients, and we pegged out the boundary.'

A couple of days later I was driving along the road and, as I passed our clients' bungalow, I noticed a pile of white pegs dumped on the grass verge.

Back in the office, I told Trevor not to bother with the bill and to put the file to the bottom of the pile.

Going Equipped

The offence of going equipped to commit burglary doesn't seem to feature in the courts these days, but as an articled clerk I was sent to sit behind Mark Carlisle on just such a case. The two defendants, both male, had been apprehended in a lane that was one of many forming a network in the countryside inland of Blackpool. The evidence against them consisted of observations by the police, to whom they were well known, and the various objects found inside their car, a grey Vauxhall, I think.

The offence took place on a summer's evening when an observant police officer had seen the two men, Ken and Norman, driving along a narrow lane that led down towards the River Wyre. He knew it was a dead end, so he radioed for help and an unmarked car arrived. When the Vauxhall emerged from the lane and turned along the main road, the police car followed at a discreet distance. The car then turned down another of the lanes that went towards the river, another dead end. The police stayed on the main road keeping watch. The Vauxhall reappeared and was driven along yet another lane, but this time the police followed and, as it reached the entrance to a large house set in extensive grounds, they indicated the Vauxhall was to pull over.

Norman and Ken got out of the car and went to meet the officers. As the two policemen, DC Smith and DC McKie, approached Norman, he pulled his wallet from the back pocket of his trousers and began searching through it.

'Here's my driving licence and I've got insurance as well,' Norman said, waving some pieces of paper under DC Smith's nose.

'Thanks,' said the officer, pushing away Norman's arm. 'Let's have a look in the car, shall we?'

All four men strode towards the car. 'What're you doing round here?' DC McKie said. He rolled his Rs and looked straight at Ken, who dropped his gaze.

'Looking for work. Been told some guy wanted a job on his roof,' Ken said.

'What's this guy's name then?' McKie said.

'Don't know, just told where he lived.'

By this time they had all reached the vehicle and the two officers opened the boot. Inside was a bag of tools, spanners, screw drivers, a couple of hammers, and laid across the base the dark metal of a crowbar glinted in the low winter sun.

'Doing a roof were we – with a crowbar.' McKie wasn't expecting an answer.

Norman spluttered. 'Yes, guv. We were going to see this guy about some work.'

'Where does he live, this bloke you were going to see?' Smith said, as he opened the front passenger door.

On the floor was a piece of paper torn from a reporter's notepad, the type anyone can buy in WH Smith's. 'We had a map …' Ken pushed past the officer, leant into the vehicle and picked up the sheet of paper. 'We'd met this guy in the pub. Said he had a few jobs we could do and he drew this map of where his house was. Here, see.' He thrust the piece of paper into DC Smith's hand.

The map had been drawn by an inexpert hand, but it clearly showed a lane off the main Cleveleys to Singleton Road. The plan showed two or three houses along a twisting lane that led down to towards the river.

DC Smith sucked his teeth as he contemplated whether to arrest the two men. He didn't believe a word they were saying, but with a good defence lawyer they would probably be acquitted. Was it worth the paperwork involved? Whatever they were up to they had been stopped in their tracks.

'Well, not sure …' he said, but was interrupted by DC McKie who was holding a book in his hand.

'What's this? A copy of *Who's Who*. Now what would you be wanting with this then?'

They were arrested and charged with going equipped with a crowbar, spanners, various tools and a copy of *Who's Who*. Despite Mr Carlisle's best endeavours both men were convicted.

Oysters and George Carman

I suppose George Carman was one of the more colourful members of the Bar and my first meeting with him was a little bizarre, to say the least. I was still an articled clerk and I was sent to Blackpool Quarter Sessions to sit behind him during a case of causing death by dangerous driving. He was a small, rather busy man, always dressed in pinstripe trousers with a black jacket and the silk waistcoat worn by QCs. The client was pleading guilty to the charge and after a rather tedious conference with him George went off to do some work in the robing room. I was left sitting with the client until, about half an hour before the midday adjournment, I was summoned to see George.

'Go and find out if there is any chance of our case coming on before lunch,' he said. I did as I was told and scurried off to find the court usher. My enquiries revealed that we were unlikely to be called before the court rose. I returned with the news to the robing room. When I told George he snorted and said, 'Damn, well, I suppose we'd better make the best of it. Do you know where Robert's Oyster Shop is on the promenade?'

It was a silly question; everyone living in Blackpool knew where to get oysters. I told him I did.

'Good. Go and tell Robert I want a dozen oysters and a pint of Guinness and tell him I'll pop in and pay later.'

I was to meet George on many occasions; there were a few other cases while I was still an articled clerk and then, when I was living in London and had become a barrister, we frequented the same drinking holes, but I was never in the same case as him again until much later on in my career.

In early 1981 I was instructed to represent a solicitor who was charged with defrauding the Legal Aid Fund of many thousands of pounds. The case was tried in Manchester and I was being led by the leader of the Northern Circuit, Mick Maguire, and George was prosecuting. As George called the various witnesses – court clerks, Law Society staff – we began to undermine the prosecution case, which was based upon a number of false premises, one of which was that a bail application would only take ten minutes of court time. That was torpedoed when a bail application was interposed in our trial; the judge said it would only take fifteen minutes at the most. It took over an hour, as Mick Maguire pointed out. George was clearly getting rattled as we scored again and again, until one lunchtime we heard him on the telephone to the Director of Public Prosecutions. 'I can take a few bullet holes below the waterline, but a bombshell is too much.'

No oysters for George that day.

A Sack of Potatoes and a
Bottle of Teepol.

Not a murder, but still one of the most interesting cases I was involved in. The client, Max, was a fisherman. He sailed in small boats out of Fleetwood when there was still a fishing fleet in the north Lancashire town. The basis that these small trawlers worked on was called 'share fishing'. The boat's owners took the major share of the profits on the catch and the remainder was split between the remaining crew.

On this trip the *Goodwill* had a crew of five. Max was the fishing skipper, the de facto captain of the ship. He wasn't a certificated captain so there was an older man on board who was, but Max really ran the boat and directed where they would sail and where they would put the nets down. He was the man with the 'nose' for the shoals.

This particular night they were fishing in the Irish Sea. One of the crew was on watch and Max had gone to his bunk to sleep. The sea was running high and the small boat rolled and pitched. It was cold and the fire in the cabin had been lit. Suddenly the boat was hit by a large wave and the gas bottle in the galley, secured in place by a sack of potatoes and a bottle of Teepol, came loose and rolled along the deck and into the cabin.

Max was awoken as the gas from the bottle exploded. He grabbed his clothes and ran through a wall of fire onto the deck. The rest of the crew had already got the lifeboat over the side and they all jumped into it. They were in the lifeboat for three days before they were picked up by another boat and taken to the Isle of Man. Here Max was treated for the burns he had suffered as he dashed from the cabin. He needed extensive skin grafts to his face and hands. He was devastatingly charming despite being very disfigured.

He sued the boat's owners for damages for the injuries he had sustained, on the basis they had failed to provide proper housing for the gas bottle in the galley. The owners raised the issue of liability at the last minute, so the case was adjourned. They claimed they were not Max's employers and did not owe a duty of care to him or the rest of the crew.

When the date came for the trial to continue, the original barrister was unavailable, so another Silk took it over only a couple of days before the hearing was due to begin. The brief ran to many pages and yet the advocate was able to read and prepare our case, no doubt sacrificing his weekend as many barristers did and still do.

The judge heard the arguments but decided that the owner of the boat was responsible for providing a safe system of work and awarded Max substantial damages. Max had shown such resilience, including obtaining his skipper's certificate, that the judge told the boat owners they were lucky because the amount by way of damages was much less than it could have been. He thought Max deserved more. The other fishermen were awarded damages as well.

I had driven them to the final hearing in my principal's car, which broke down on the way back. Fortunately my passengers were too elated to worry about the delay caused and waited patiently at the roadside until we were rescued by the AA.

A Solicitor

I qualified as a solicitor and was admitted to the role on 15th June 1971. Almost immediately I was instructed to go to the Blackpool office where I would be working in the future. Articled clerks were the lowest of the low and now I was qualified I would have a secretary and clerks who would be answerable to me, so the senior partner believed I needed to be with different staff. I was to be the second advocate in the local magistrates' courts, doing family work and some personal injuries cases as well.

Within weeks of me qualifying the partner who did most of the advocacy for the firm announced he was leaving to set up his own practice. The partners at Ingham Clegg and Crowther told him to leave immediately. I was asked to take over his work, which meant I was doing all the work in the magistrates' court. Some years later I was told I was the first female solicitor to appear in the Blackpool Magistrates' Court.

I moved into the partner's office and had my own secretary, who occupied a small room next to me. She took all my telephone calls and filtered them. One police officer was overheard saying that trying to speak to me was like trying to get through to Buckingham Palace.

The senior partner's younger daughter was assigned to work with me. She was a feisty young lady and one day burst into my office, when I was seeing a client, with a copy of *Cosmopolitan* open at the centre-page spread of a naked Burt Reynolds.

Discretion Statement

Before the law on divorce altered in the early 1970s the petitioner – the person seeking the divorce – had to establish one of a number of matrimonial offences. Cruelty, adultery, or separation for two years were the main causes I remember. And because it was an equitable relief, the clue is in the word petitioner, the husband or wife seeking the divorce had to come to the court 'with clean hands'. In practice, this caused a lot of problems; very often the petitioner was in another relationship and so the courts established a procedure whereby the petitioner asked the court to grant their petition for a divorce notwithstanding their own adultery. A sealed envelope would be handed to the judge detailing the adultery; this was known as a discretion statement.

Soon after I qualified as a solicitor I had just such a case. The wife, Helen Broad, was a glamorous blonde, and she had left her husband and was living with another man. She and I discussed at length how to deal with her discretion statement and we agreed on a wording that essentially said she had entered into another relationship and had committed adultery on numerous occasions over the preceding two years. The statement was signed by her and placed in a sealed envelope.

On the day of the hearing of Helen Broad's petition, we met the barrister I had instructed to appear on her behalf, Cedric Fox, in the waiting area of the County Court. He towered over both me and the client as I introduced her to him.

Helen was wearing a pale camel coat, her long blonde hair was loose, and her lips were painted a bright red. She was the best-looking woman in the room. Cedric took her hand and held on to it for a little longer than necessary, before directing us to a quiet corner where he could discuss the case and try to put Helen at ease.

Cedric manoeuvred his not inconsiderable bulk down onto a chair and pulled it up close to where we were sitting.

'Is there a discretion statement?' he said.

I searched through my file and handed him the brown envelope containing the carefully crafted disclosure. He opened it, his heavy fingers tearing the paper apart and, rather more carefully, took out the piece of paper inside. He fished his glasses out of the top pocket of his dark pinstriped suit and began to read. The petitioner watched him, her mouth in a wide smile, but the eyes suggested she was a little wary.

Cedric looked over the top of his glasses. 'Don't you know how many times you have committed adultery?'

Helen Broad looked him straight in the face and said, 'I don't count, do you?'

A Thwarted Fireman

Arson is a frightening offence; smoke and flames can not only cause enormous damage but the risk to lives is always present. Early in my legal career a fire at one of the public houses in Blackpool caused extensive damage to the premises and meant the doors were closed for days in the middle of the holiday season. Fortunately no one was hurt.

When the police investigated it became obvious that the publican's son had watched the blaze and taken photographs of the fire appliances. He was identified as the main suspect.

As the enquiry continued the sergeant in charge found a scrap book, which contained photographs taken at the scene of other fires in the Blackpool area, newspaper cuttings about other cases of arson, and a broken footplate from a fire engine. The publican's son was arrested and interviewed under caution, during which, although he at first denied setting the fire, eventually he admitted he was the culprit. He was charged and I was instructed to represent him.

When the fire broke out the defendant's parents were not in the property but his grandmother was, and because of that he was charged with arson with intent to endanger life. The fire was attended by three fire engines and put the lives of a large number of firemen at risk.

My recollection of the young man is that he was in his twenties at the time of the offence, having left school at sixteen. He wanted to join the fire brigade, but he was too young. When he reached eighteen he made an application, but it was refused. He continued to make a number of applications to both

Blackpool and Lancashire fire brigades but was never successful.

He was obsessed with fires and turned up whenever and wherever the local fire engines were working. He had set the fire at the public house so that he could watch the fire brigade arrive and fight the fire.

The case was heard at the Lancaster Crown Court before a High Court judge. He pleaded guilty and when the police sergeant was called to give evidence of the defendant's previous convictions he took a very unusual step. When prosecuting counsel indicated he had no more questions for the officer, the detective sergeant turned to the judge and said, 'My lord, I do want to say that during the course of the investigation I have spent time talking to the defendant's grandmother. She is not well and I believe if the defendant was sent to prison it would hasten her death.'

The judge listened carefully to what the officer said and the other mitigation put forward by defence counsel. When he passed sentence he explained to the defendant that the sentence for arson with intent to endanger life was a period in prison, but because of the unusual plea made by the policeman on his behalf he would pass a sentence that allowed the defendant to return to his family within a matter of weeks.

The Mandie Queen

The cell under the courtrooms at Blackpool was bare, the walls and floor the dull grey of unpainted concrete. There was no furniture. In the corner of the room, crouched down, his head touching his knees and rocking to and fro, was my client, David W. He was dressed in a curious mix of ill-fitting clothes garnered from some corners of the police station. His own had been taken for examination by forensic scientists. The door of the cell closed with the thud of heavy metal behind me and for a moment the rocking ceased as he looked in my direction.

'I loved her. Why would I kill her?'

'Do you want to tell me about it?' I said.

The rocking began again. As I waited, I thought about David's wife, Lynn, a thin, anxious woman in her early twenties and known locally as the Mandie Queen, on account of her swallowing Mandrax tablets like they were sweets. Her body had been found three days previously, lying naked on their bed in a rundown holiday flat on Blackpool's South Shore. The pathologist said she had died as a result of vagal inhibition when pressure was applied to her neck. That assault had resulted in the hyoid bone in her neck being fractured. Although her blood contained a high level of the illegal drugs, they had not been the cause of death, indeed the pathologist asserted the level was insufficient to have killed her.

David continued to insist he had not murdered her. He said they had both smoked some cannabis and taken other illegally obtained drugs.

'She was totally out of it. She wanted me to go and get something to eat. She wouldn't shut up. I went down to the corner shop. I bought some bread and some other things.'

I knew he had bought some ham and milk because the police had found those items on the worktop together with a receipt.

'I got back to the flat. Lynn was on the bed with the covers over her. I thought she was asleep. I tried to wake her up. I couldn't. I got hold of her wrist. She didn't have a pulse. She wasn't breathing. I looked at her tabs. She'd taken some more. We had a stash of drugs hidden. I decided to get rid of them. I was going to call the police but wanted to get rid of them first.'

'Why didn't you call the police?' I said.

'I panicked. Decided to run for it.' His face was stained with tears. 'I loved her, why would I kill her?'

I didn't tell him that I was aware he had been violent towards her in the past. Lynn had been to see me a few weeks previously, asking me to represent her in divorce proceedings. I had immediately told her I couldn't do so as David was already my client, so I didn't hear what she was complaining about, but a large bruise under her left eye had told me all I needed to know.

I stood on the other side of the cell watching him rocking back and forth. It wasn't really the image I had of a murderer. In my imagination they were tough, brutish, large men with snarling faces, a fairy-tale thug, not this disturbed young man with a pale thin face and long dark curly hair who looked more like Prince Charming than a killer.

David maintained his plea of not guilty and the case was heard at Lancaster Assizes in the same courtroom where the Pendle witches were tried over four hundred years ago. The only issue in the trial was the cause of death; was she strangled or did she die of an overdose? The pathologist I had instructed took the view that the evidence of strangulation was weak, but when he gave evidence, he accused the Home Office pathologist of breaking the hyoid bone in a clumsy dissection. At that point,, the QC representing David advised him to plead guilty to manslaughter and he agreed to do so. He was sentenced to serve six years in prison, some of which he served at Parkhurst on the Isle of Wight, where his brother was serving a sentence for armed robbery.

A few years later the doctor we had instructed to give evidence about the effects of taking large quantities of methaqualone, the active ingredient of Mandrax tablets, sent me a paper published in a scientific journal which argued that the level of methaqualone in the kidneys was a better indication of poisoning than that in the bloodstream. The level in Lynn's kidneys was over the safe limit described in the paper. Did David kill his wife? Perhaps not.

I rather hope he wasn't responsible for her death, because only three months previously he had faced a charge of possession of illegal amphetamines in the magistrates' court. I had secured a not guilty verdict on a technicality. Had he been convicted he would have gone to prison because he was in breach of a suspended sentence. And Lynn might not have died.

On a Knife Edge

I received the telephone call at about nine o'clock one evening. The police officer on the other end of the phone asked me if I could come to the station in Blackpool immediately. He went on to tell me they had woman in custody and they thought she should speak to a solicitor. This was before the days of the Police and Criminal Evidence Act 1976 and asking any lawyer to see a prisoner before they were interviewed and charged was unusual.

'It's a serious case. She's stabbed her husband and he's in surgery at the moment. If he dies …' His voice trailed off, leaving me to deduce she would probably be charged with murder.

When I arrived at the police station in central Blackpool, I was shown into a cell where I saw Eleanor for the first time. She was in her late thirties, dressed in a tweed skirt and a thin blue sweater. Sitting upright on the edge of the concrete shelf that served as a bed, she was twisting and turning a white handkerchief in her hands. Her wedding ring caught the light from the single unshaded bulb.

'Is there any news?' she said.

I shook my head and said, 'No, not yet.' Before she could say anything further I sat down next to her and introduced myself.

'Yes, the solicitor. They told me you were coming.' She continued to turn the handkerchief over. 'I didn't mean to kill him.'

'We don't know that you have.' I took hold of her hand.

'We had such a row. He'd come in late the night before. Playing football. More likely down the pub. I'd had his supper waiting for him since six. He said he didn't want it. He went to work this morning, whistling away to himself. I was very annoyed with him. He came home at midday and I gave him the meal I'd prepared the previous night. What's this, he said? I told him, it's your dinner. He went mad and was swearing at me, then he picked up the plate and threw it at the wall. I went over and grabbed his arm. He shook me off and ran upstairs, pulled my clothes out of the wardrobe and started ripping them. I tried to get hold of him but he pushed me away and went back downstairs. I followed and he told me to get out of the house. He opened the front door and tried to force me to leave. I told him I wasn't going and ran into the kitchen. That's where it happened. We were struggling, throwing pots and pans at each other. He was shouting at me to leave and I was screaming. I was backed up against the table and I reached back and the bread knife was there. I picked it up and thrust it at him.'

She began to sob. 'That's when the police officers rushed in and they took him away.'

I had been told that two off-duty officers had been passing when they heard the sounds of a fight coming from the house. They'd rushed in and seen Eleanor's husband with the handle of a knife protruding from his stomach. They realised he would not survive the wait for an ambulance so they carried him to their car and while one drove to the hospital, the other held the knife in place and tried to staunch the flow of blood from the wound.

Eleanor continued to sob and I sat and held her hand. A police woman brought us cups of tea as we waited for news. A little later another officer came and gave us a couple of blankets. I still had my coat, so I tucked one blanket round her legs and the other over her shoulders. From time to time she still shivered. I pulled my coat round me.

Eventually, in the early hours of the morning, the officer who had summoned me to the police station came into the cell.

'He's out of theatre and he's going to live,' he said.

Eleanor, who had stood up when he came into the cell, sank back onto the bed, bent over and began to weep. I picked up the blanket and wrapped it round her again.

'I think I'll get matron. Perhaps she can give you something,' the officer said. 'Miss Barnes will want to go.'

'I'll see you tomorrow,' I said.

Matron bustled in and took over. I left the cell with the officer and when I was satisfied I could not be overheard by Eleanor I said, 'Will you charge her?'

'Yes, attempted murder. I assume you'll be in court tomorrow.'

'Yes,' I said.

Eleanor was lucky. Not only did her husband survive the assault but after she pleaded guilty he begged the judge to be merciful and she was given a suspended sentence.

But I received no payment for the night I spent in the cells.

The Drop Room

Custody disputes are distressing. There are no winners and the children are usually the ones who suffer most. Today, courts do their best to ensure that no child is upset by the proceedings and very few attend court, their views being placed before the judge by a social worker. But, at the start of my career, contested custody cases were heard by a High Court judge and there were no special arrangements for children.

My client, Sarah, was disputing the custody of her two children, a boy of ten and a girl of eight. Since the divorce they had been living with their father. He worked and they spent a great deal of time with their grandparents, neither of whom enjoyed the best of health. That was the basis for Sarah's claim for custody of her children.

She was a strange character. A tall blonde who always wore dark glasses because, she claimed, of some medical condition. This was her second divorce, although to be fair to her, her first marriage had not lasted very long and there were no children. She had left her first husband for the man she then married and who was the father of the two children.

This marriage had lasted twelve years, but then she had found another man. She decided to leave her husband and her children for this new relationship. That didn't last very long and now she wanted her children back. I, rather cynically, thought she was more interested in the maintenance than the welfare of her son and daughter.

When the court's children's officer spoke to them they said they wanted to tell the judge they wished to stay with their dad. I advised

Sarah that she should withdraw her application for custody as I believed the judge would not go against their wishes. The lapse of time – they had been with their father for over a year – was against her as well. She insisted the hearing should go ahead because she thought the children were being pressurised by their father.

The hearing was at Lancaster Assizes. The High Court judge was on circuit and was sitting in the court inside the castle. This case was to be heard not in the courtroom, which looked like it was the set for a horror movie, but in the judge's chambers. We waited outside the room in a narrow corridor, all of us crushed together – the grandparents, Sarah, her ex-husband – all trying to avoid each other's eyes. The children had been brought by the social worker. They ignored their mother's smiles.

The door to the judge's chambers was opened by a very tall and slender young man with lank fair hair, dressed in a morning suit: the judge's marshal, probably a would-be barrister. He stood to one side and waved us into the room. He introduced the case in a rather high-pitched voice. I had to suppress a smile at the thought that his voice hadn't broken.

The judge was sitting at his desk in the centre of the room. His robes lay over a chair and his wig was on the desk looking like a dead animal. The room was quite large, with windows that overlooked the Priory Church and a small square. One of those windows was the size of a door, with a small step in front of it.

'Come and stand here,' the judge said to the two children. They inched forward, eyes wide open.

'Now, do you know what this room is called?'

They shook their heads, their eyes fixed on the judge.

'It's called the Drop Room. And can you guess why it's called that?'

Again they shook their heads. *Oh no*, I thought. I knew what he was about to say.

'You see that window there?'

This time they nodded but their eyes were even wider and they stared at the window.

'You see it's got a step up?'

Their faces were rigid and they tipped their heads down.

'They used to hang people from there. Pushed them out of the window with a rope round their necks.'

The children's faces were white.

'Well, that's not going to happen to you. Now, I understand you want to tell me about where you want to live.'

The little boy stuttered, 'With Dad.'

The judge looked at the girl. 'And you?'

She took her brother's hand and nodded but couldn't speak.

Not surprisingly the judge awarded custody of the two traumatised children to the father.

A Brown Paper Package

Legal privilege is often misunderstood. Any client, no matter who he is or what he tells you, is entitled to confidentiality. The question I had to deal with was whether that extended to property that may be required by the police as evidence in a criminal case.

The problem arose when the wife and co-defendant in a case of conspiracy to supply drugs came to my office and handed me a brown paper parcel, which I was asked to keep on her husband's behalf. Adrian was a low-level drug dealer in Blackpool and south Lancashire. He had a team of young men who sold the drugs he supplied on the streets and he had devised a rather simple but effective system of getting his money. He had opened a number of Post Office accounts in fictitious names into which his runners could pay the proceeds of sale. When he wanted money he used these accounts. The police knew from the suppliers they had arrested that Adrian was the source of the drugs, but the only evidence against him was what these accomplices had said. There was no direct evidence. The evidence of an accomplice usually requires some corroboration if a jury is to rely on it, and that's if they can be persuaded to attend court. Not surprisingly the police were desperate to find some way of linking Adrian to these accounts and from them to the supply of drugs.

Adrian was arrested and interviewed but he refused to answer any questions. I should say that this too was before the Police and Criminal Evidence Act 1976, which gave a suspected person the right to have a solicitor present during interviews. I saw him in the cells for the first time just before I made a bail application on his behalf. Despite the fact that the police had no evidence against him except the statements under caution of co-accused in the conspiracy, the magistrates agreed to the prosecution application for him to be remanded in custody.

For the next few weeks there was stalemate. Adrian was produced every week to be remanded yet again as the police made numerous enquiries to locate the post offices where money had been deposited and link those accounts to Adrian. Searches of the flat where Adrian lived, his parents' address and their caravan in the Lake District failed to unearth the passbooks.

Although they couldn't interview him because he had been charged with the offence, they put some pressure on his wife, who at that stage had not been charged. In addition, they contacted me to ask about the whereabouts of the Post Office account books. I told them I couldn't help.

After about five or six weeks, Adrian's wife came into my office with a brown parcel and said her husband had requested I keep the package. I didn't open it or ask what it contained, although I had a pretty shrewd idea. I did ask for assurance that it didn't contain anything that was explosive or could catch fire.

Twenty-four hours later, the chief inspector and his sidekick, a rather nasty sergeant I had had previous dealings with, presented themselves in my office and threatened to arrest me and charge me with perverting the course of justice by withholding evidence. I told them I had done no such thing and said they were to arrest me and charge me if they had any evidence to that effect. They informed me they knew I had a package that contained vital evidence in the case against Adrian. I responded by telling them my client's affairs were subject to legal privilege. And I repeated they should show me any evidence they had to prove their assertion I was acting illegally. When they couldn't, and repeated their threats, I asked them to leave. After a few minutes of them haranguing me without any success they got up and left.

I wasn't as sure of myself as I had represented and once they had left I spoke to my senior partner, who was supportive. I then rang the Law Society who confirmed that my interpretation of the law was correct and the parcel was covered by my client's legal privilege.

Adrian continued to use the parcel to good effect and in exchange for the contents of the package they agreed not to oppose an application for bail. The parcel was handed over and as I suspected contained about twenty Post Office passbooks showing the transactions Adrian had made. He had done a good deal with the police because the prosecution agreed to accept pleas of guilty to a number of offences of supplying drugs, rather than a conspiracy, thereby reducing the length of time he would spend in custody; the case against his wife was dropped.

The Move to London

On August bank holiday Monday 1973 I had to attend court for an urgent bail application. It was a beautiful day and I hopped into my car, a Triumph Spitfire I had bought the day I qualified. The hood was down and I began my journey to the court, about a mile away. The roads were very busy as families made their way to the beaches and promenade of the famous seaside resort. Halfway along I found myself following the grey rear ends of a string of donkeys also heading for the beach. I didn't want to be there.

I enjoyed working for Ingham Clegg and Crowther. They had been generous employers and during my articles allowed me to learn about every aspect of a solicitors' practice. My colleagues were fun to work with and there was a great sense of camaraderie. However, the north of England was still very chauvinistic and too many men found working for or with a woman unacceptable.

A few days before the bank holiday I had a telephone conversation with a police officer who asked on several occasions to speak to the solicitor dealing with the accused, refusing to accept my assertion that I was a solicitor and he had to speak to me. There were also barriers to my career prospects, including a senior partner who told me I was sure to get married and leave the practice. I believe in time I would have overcome these hurdles, but I was young and impatient.

London beckoned with all its intensity and complexity so, like many before me, I went south.

A Question of Tactics

West London courthouse was in Southcombe Street, W14; it was a red-brick building with an impressive entrance in white stone. On the floor of the entrance hall was a mosaic of the Metropolitan Police crest, a reminder that this had been known as a police court when it first opened. The name may have been changed but the court was still run by police officers. They organised the list of defendants and had an office where they collected the fines imposed by the magistrates.

At the back of the main hall was a door marked 'Police Only'. This led to a small room on one side and a corridor of cells where defendants were held while they waited for their cases to be called and, after a hearing, for the prison van to arrive.

Solicitors were allowed into the cell area to take instructions, standing by the wicket gate to talk to their client. The other room was the province of the police matron who dispensed cups of tea for a small sum. It was here that, if you had made friends with the local CID, you would be given a brief outline of the evidence against a client. There was no practice of serving statements in cases that were to be heard by the magistrates. Only if the case was being committed to the Crown Court would a lawyer get to see the evidence against the defendant.

One of the warrant officers, a man known as Jock, was a caricature of a Scotsman, quite tall, balding with a fringe of red hair, and a ferocious temper. His role was to run the list for the court. When defendants arrived at the courthouse, whether on bail or brought by the prison van, they were ticked off on the sheets kept by the warrant officer. A defendant's lawyer would, after seeing their client, tell the officer what application they would be making to the magistrate. The policeman would then decide the order in which cases would be called, usually depending on the kind of application. Adjournments where there were no applications usually went first, then applications for bail, and pleas in mitigation were left to the end. Solicitors were always keen to get their cases on as soon as possible; there was always more work to be done in the office, or another court to attend.

Jock tended to favour local solicitors when deciding the order in which to call cases into court; barristers and out-of-area solicitors were usually put to the back. However, if for some reason you offended him, your case would be put down the list. It was often difficult to know what you had done to upset him. Not being deferential enough was perhaps the most common offence, but there were others. I soon learnt that the best way of getting my cases on first was to make sure I upset him as early as possible. My cases would go to the bottom of the list, but by the time the hearing began, I could guarantee that other lawyers would also have committed some error and their cases too would be transferred to the bottom and, in the process, my clients would get nearer the top. Just a question of tactics.

The Man in the White Suit

I am not referring to the journalist Martin Bell, who stood for Parliament some years ago, but to a solicitor who had an office close to West London Magistrates' Court. This was before it moved to the shadow of the Hammersmith Flyover. I had only just started working for another local solicitors' practice as the second-string advocate when the outdoor clerk, a Welsh lady who liked a drink or two, or maybe three, told me I needed to meet Bob.

'He's really good looking, and single,' she said, acknowledging my own status. And so he was: six feet tall, a mop of dark hair, and a sonorous voice with just a trace of an accent I recognised as being like my own. He was one of the many Lancastrians who had moved to London hoping to make their fortune or at least a decent living in the big city.

When the court doors opened in the morning, the outdoor clerk would dash across the road to see if any of our regular clients were in the cells and to try and get our share of the unrepresented prisoners. She would then come back into the office and prepare a list of the cases we had to cover. There were two courtrooms in the building; I was meant to do the shorter list, usually with the less serious cases, and the main advocate would do the more important ones. It never seemed to work out that way and I found myself covering most of the work in both courts, which brought me into contact with the 'man in the white suit'.

It wasn't his usual choice of dress; he normally wore a grey or navy blue pinstripe, but sometimes in the summer, and when he wanted to make a dramatic entrance, he wore white. I liked Bob, but quickly worked out that he was not the man for me; he was far too eccentric.

However, we worked well together in the courtroom even though we were competitors for business. A long list of clients meant there was too little time to see them all before the stipendiary magistrate came into court. Bob and I learnt to work the list officer so that our cases were not listed consecutively, and this allowed a little time to see a client who had not yet appeared.

Cases in the magistrates' court can be very amusing, and West London had its quota of drunks – homeless men who lived on and around Shepherd's Bush Green. They were usually brought before the court for being drunk and disorderly and, although we wouldn't be paid, both Bob and I often addressed the court on their behalf.

One man, whose age was impossible to tell from his appearance he was so unkempt, in a dirty mac, torn green sweater and a once-white shirt, was before the court for stealing a tin of salmon. He was one of Bob's clients and this was one of the white suit days.

The defendant pleaded guilty to the theft and Bob stood up to mitigate on his behalf. He was immediately interrupted by the magistrate. 'Your client has been in prison too many times. What am I going to do with him? Send him back for a tin of salmon?'

'That's exactly what I am asking you to do, your worship. The last time he was in custody, he got his teeth seen to. The upper jaw. He'd like to go back to get his lower ones sorted out. That's why he stole the tin of salmon. He needs a sentence of a least three months for the prison service to sort that out,' said Bob.

He got his three months. Whether he got his teeth sorted out I don't know, because that winter he died of exposure, and it was Bob and me, together with the list officer, who organised a whip-round to pay for his funeral.

The Stipendiary Magistrate

During my time in Blackpool I had only appeared in front of lay magistrates, those upstanding members of the local community the Lord Chancellor's Department thought were fit and proper persons to dispense justice to their fellow citizens. They often lacked any real understanding of the law and sometimes struggled to assimilate the facts of a case, but I am sure they did their best. Often they had unqualified staff as court clerks who didn't know the law either. That has all changed now and court clerks have to be qualified lawyers if they are advising the bench of lay magistrates on legal matters, and the justices of the peace are given much more thorough training.

My move to live in London brought me into contact with a different kind of JP, the stipendiary magistrate. They were a fearsome bunch and, at first, I was a little in awe of them. Over ninety per cent of all criminal cases are dealt with in the magistrates' courts and the stipendiary magistrates, whether solicitors or barristers, were much quicker at dealing with them and expected those appearing in their court to be brief.

St John Harmsworth sat at the court in Marlborough Street in the heart of the West End, next to the London Palladium and just across the road from Liberty's. He was extremely punctual, walking briskly into court dressed in a pinstripe suit, a military tie of navy blue and dark red stripes, and a fresh rose in his buttonhole. If he was strict in his interpretation of the law, he was also humane.

One morning I was sitting in court waiting for my case to be called on, when a fifty-year-old was brought into the dock. He had been charged with being drunk and disorderly. The arresting officer (they went to court then) stood in the witness box and said he had stopped the defendant because he been staggering about on Oxford Street at about eight o'clock that very morning.

'I spoke to him to ask his name, sir, and noticed his breath smelt of alcohol, his speech was slurred and he was unsteady on his feet, sir,' the policeman said. This was the formula all officers used when describing somebody as drunk.

The warrant officer, the man who controls the order the cases are called before the bench, moved forward. 'He was only released from Pentonville this morning, sir.'

'What time were you released from custody?' said St John Harmsworth, addressing the man in the dock.

'Six, sir.'

'How did you manage to get drunk between six and eight?'

'Well, Your Honour …' (Defendants in the magistrates' court frequently get the form of address wrong. Only Crown Court judges are addressed as Your Honour.) 'It's my birthday, see, and the lads in the kitchen at Pentonville brewed some hooch and we spent the night like, well, drinking.'

St John Harmsworth looked at the charge sheet in front of him. 'So it is. Well, as it's your birthday I'll fine you five pounds or one day,' he said. There was no need to explain to the defendant that the one day meant he was to stay in custody for the remainder of the court day. It was a common way of dealing with those whose offences were minor and means were limited.

As the prisoner was being led away the learned magistrate said to the warrant officer, 'Release him as soon as he's sobered up.'

In these changing times I was a little sad to see Marlborough Street magistrates court had been transformed into a boutique hotel.

Scarves by the Yard

I was not a natural prosecutor but paying the bills meant I did do some when I was first called to the Bar. I went to Marlborough Street magistrates court frequently, mainly prosecuting women arrested for theft in the stores on Oxford Street. At that time the shops themselves brought the prosecutions and the main witness would be a store detective who had observed the offender taking goods without paying for them. The alleged thief would then be stopped as they left the store and taken back to an office. The store detective would call the police and when a police officer arrived the suspect would be formally arrested.

On this occasion the store detective had seen a woman take a silk scarf from a display and drop it into the large shopping bag she was carrying. The detective continued to observe the woman as she moved around the counter of scarves from expensive fashion houses. The woman repeated the action a few times, hiding each scarf in her bag. After about ten minutes she went into a different department and, although she picked up other items, she didn't take any of them. Eventually she bought a piece of jewellery and then left the store. The store detective stopped her. 'Would you please come back into the store. I believe you have something you haven't paid for.'

'Have I? I've just bought this.' The woman produced the bag containing the item of jewellery.

'I'd like you to come back to the office with me.'

The woman shrugged her shoulders. 'I'm sure I've paid for everything.'

In the office the store detective called the police. While they waited for an officer to arrive, the woman turned out the contents of her handbag. Amongst them was the receipt for the jewellery and her wallet, which contained a variety of credit cards and over five hundred pounds in cash. 'Why would I steal anything when I have all this money?'

'Let's just wait for the police, shall we.'

When the officer arrived, the store detective described what she had seen and the policewoman cautioned the suspect. The woman became very agitated. 'I haven't taken anything.'

'Shall we look in your bags,' the policewoman said.

The woman emptied her handbag again and put the large shopping bag onto the desk. The policewoman opened the large bag and pulled from it a silk scarf. 'What's this?'

'It must have fallen into my bag when I was looking at them. Let me pay for it, please. I have money. Look.' She held out her wallet. 'Card or cash. Which do you want?'

'I think we'll go to the station,' the policewoman said.

When they got to the police station the woman began to sob and pleaded to pay for the scarf. The procedure for checking her into the custody suite took some time but eventually they found an interview room and the officer prepared to question the woman. The suspect was wriggling on her seat. 'I want to go to the toilet.'

'Can it wait until we've finished?'

'No, no. I want to go now.'

The policewoman wasn't convinced the woman was making a genuine request. 'I'll go with you.'

As they walked towards the toilet the woman was walking awkwardly as if she had something between her legs. At the door of the toilet she tried to push the officer away. The officer held the door partly open, enabling the woman to have some privacy if her request was genuine. After a moment or two the police officer realised the woman was not sitting on the toilet seat but was pulling something from under her skirt.

'Ok, let's have a look at what you've got there.'

When a search was made of the woman's underwear about ten scarves by fashion houses such as Chanel and Hermès were found. The cost of them was over a thousand pounds.

Battered Wives

Soon after I moved to London I was asked by the Cambridge Settlement if I would help a group of women who were trying to establish a Battered Wives Refuge in the East End of London. They needed a woman lawyer; the group did not want a man coming into the house, and there wasn't a lawyer amongst the Cambridge graduates.

The group had identified a suitable property, a former doctor's house and surgery on East India Dock Road. One night I found myself, a respectable member of the legal profession, along with four other women, climbing the wall of these premises and breaking into the house though a side window. After making it habitable, getting the electricity connected and arranging to pay the rates, a number of women with their children came to live there.

I had been recruited to assist the women with their legal proceedings, and there were a number of social workers who worked with the families to help with claiming benefits and arranging schools and accommodation away from the area. The house had room for about ten women and we had set out a number of rules about how the house would run, such as a cleaning rota, use of bathrooms and the kitchen. In order to ensure the house continued to run effectively, we decided to have a weekly meeting at which any problems could be aired, and I would make appointments to see anyone who needed help. Sometimes that was as simple as explaining letters they had received from their own lawyer or advising them on the quite complicated legal choices they would need to make.

Generally things went well, until one woman came to the house with her three children. She was very difficult, the children were always filthy, and she left the kitchen in a mess, preferring to spend time watching television. Her husband turned up frequently to ask if the children were alright. I formed the view that the women was, to a large extent, the author of her own misfortunes. I said as much to one of the social workers who retorted that there was never an excuse for violence.

Our meetings were always held at seven thirty on a Monday evening in the sitting room, the only shared space in the house. One evening, as we all gathered, this woman came in and turned on the television, pronouncing that she didn't want to attend the meeting but wanted to watch *EastEnders*. The social worker who had told me there was never any reason to assault another person asked her to turn the TV off. When she refused, the social worker went over to the TV and switched it off. The woman got up and turned it back on. This was repeated a number of times with the language getting more heated until, as the woman stepped forward again towards the TV, the social worker grabbed hold of her by the arm, swung her round and slapped her face.

The Rapist from Iran

Although I have been in close proximity to quite a number of very violent men, I have only been assaulted twice in the course of my work. The first time was while I was still working as a solicitor and had been instructed to represent an Iranian man who was charged with a number of rapes. He was in his late twenties and, when I first met him, was quite charming. Because of the seriousness of the offences I instructed a QC to defend him.

The allegations divided into two groups. The first two were made by the same young woman, who said she had met the defendant in Covent Garden where he had told her he was a student, newly arrived in London, and knew no one. She took pity on him and at the end of the evening she invited him to her flat.

It was there that he had forced himself upon her on two occasions, despite her resistance. His case was that she was a willing participant in the sexual activity. My client had left the flat the next morning and despite the police being called immediately they were unable to apprehend him.

The second set of offences was similar but took place a few months later. Again, he had met a young woman who took pity on him and invited him back to her flat. What he was unaware of was that she was living with a female partner who returned to the flat later that night and found the defendant there with her lover, who was clearly very distressed. The partner called the police and he was arrested while running away from the premises.

We made an application to sever the two sets of allegations and to our surprise the judge granted it. My client was acquitted of the first group of rapes but was convicted of the second. His defence that the woman had consented was not believed by the jury, not least because her sexual preferences were quite clear. He was sentenced to seven years in prison.

Immediately after being sentenced he was held at Wormwood Scrubs and soon I began to receive letters from him telling me he wanted to appeal against his conviction. We had already told him he had no grounds to appeal when we saw him in the cells below the Old Bailey, but despite that oral opinion and knowing, as I did, that no appeal was possible, I obtained a written advice from the Silk in the case. I forwarded that to the client and hoped that was the last of it.

A week or two elapsed and then the letters started again, begging me to file grounds of appeal. I ignored them. One day, after I had been in court, I returned to the office to find, amongst the usual list of telephone calls to which I needed to respond, a message from the probation officer at the Scrubs. I returned his call and he asked me to come and see my client and explain why he was unable to appeal. I agreed somewhat reluctantly to see him the next time I was at the prison, which I knew was only a matter of a couple of days hence.

Once in the interview room I repeated the opinion of the QC and tried to explain why learned counsel thought the verdict was not appealable, in as simple language as I could muster. The client became very angry and told me I was nothing more than a whore because I did not cover my legs and my head. I told him I was leaving. By this time he was screaming abuse at me and as I stood up to leave he lunged across the table at me and grabbed me by one arm. He didn't get any further because the prison officers had heard him shouting and they seized hold of him by the scruff of his neck and dragged him away from me.

It was a distressing experience and I needed a stiff drink that night.

A Sad, Sad Case

Over the years I must have seen hundreds of defendants, but there are very few whose faces I can visualise now. One I can wasn't even my client. I was sitting in court number 2 at West London Magistrates', waiting for my case to be called on, when a young man probably aged around twenty was guided into court by a police officer. He was quite tall and of a sturdy build; his black hair was curled so tightly that his scalp was visible. In profile his nose was straight without any hint of his African ancestry. His clothes were scruffy; a pale blue shirt hung out of his ripped jeans and his trainers looked as if they were a size too small. Despite it still being early spring he had no jumper and no coat with him.

He was before the court for the offence of 'being in possession of an offensive weapon'. A police officer got in the witness box and described to the court finding the young male in the recess of a shop door, sitting on the floor clutching to his body a large stick, which the officer produced. The stick looked like the branch of a small tree, a few inches in diameter and twisted.

Had he threatened anyone with the stick, the magistrate asked.

'No,' said the policeman.

'Is it adapted in any way, for example a nail in one end, or sharpened to make it into a weapon?'

'No,' said the officer.

'Did the defendant say anything to show why he had this stick?'

'When I arrested and cautioned him …' The policeman held his notebook up and read from it: 'It's my only friend.'

Throughout the proceedings the young man was totally passive, his eyes looking inward as if there was no future to see. His lawyer got to her feet, but the magistrate said she didn't need to address the bench because he and his colleagues were going to dismiss the charge, but not before the probation officer had spoken to the defendant and arrangements had been made for him to go to a suitable hospital.

I doubt he would be treated so well now; there is such a shortage of places for the mentally ill in our hospitals and that young man needed a place where he felt secure and would be treated appropriately.

Paying the Price

I have already said that sitting in a magistrates court waiting for your case to come on can be very entertaining. I was doing just that at Bow Street when a man was brought before the magistrate for an offence of indecent behaviour in a Royal Park. The man had picked up a prostitute on Park Lane and they had gone into Hyde Park to complete the transaction. A policeman had caught them in *delicto flagrante* under a tree.

'I allowed them time to straighten their dress, which was in some disarray, and then arrested them,' the officer said, with the sort of straight face only a police officer in court can muster. The man pleaded guilty and the magistrate imposed a fine, warning him that the consequences would be more severe if he was caught again, and may result in him having to explain to his wife where he was and why.

The next person in the dock was the prostitute. She had a long list of previous convictions for soliciting in a public place, but the magistrate was reluctant to do anything other than fine her. When he told her how much she would have to pay, she asked for time to do so.

'Have you no money with you?' the magistrate asked.

'No.'

The court officer confirmed she had only a few coins in her possession and a return ticket to Birmingham where she lived. She was one of a number of women who came to London and solicited on Park Lane by the hotels in order to supplement their benefit.

'Did you not get paid last night?' the magistrate said.

'No, sir.'

'Has Mr X gone?' said the magistrate to the court officer.

The policeman put his head round the door to the custody area, turned back and said, 'He's still here, sir.'

'Right, bring him back.'

Mr X was led back into the courtroom, somewhat bemused, and stood facing the magistrate.

'You didn't pay her last night,' the magistrate said, nodding towards the woman in the dock.

'No, there wasn't time.'

'Well, there is now. You'll pay her fine.'

And with that both were dismissed from the courtroom.

Defending the Guilty

One of the most frequently asked questions of any lawyer is 'How do you defend someone you know is guilty?' The answer is it's nothing to do with me. I'm just an advocate; only a judge and jury can decide someone is guilty. Of course, it's not as simple as that. If a client tells their lawyer they are guilty, except in very particular circumstances the lawyer cannot defend them. If, however, they insist they are innocent, then no matter how strong the evidence is against them, the advocate's duty is to put their client's case to the best of their ability.

Usually, if on the basis of the evidence I have, the case looks overwhelming, I would advise the client to plead guilty to the offence because doing so will probably result in him getting a less severe sentence. Sometimes that can result in the barrister or solicitor being sacked by the client. Very early on in my career, I learnt to be careful about the amount of pressure I put on a defendant who insisted he was innocent in the face of very convincing evidence.

The client was a juvenile and, because of his age, the trial was to take place in the Juvenile Court. At that time the prosecution, in this case the Metropolitan Police Solicitors, were under no obligation to serve any of the witness statements. Usually the police officer would provide a brief summary of the evidence to the lawyers involved.

The charge against my client was one of arson. I was told that the fire had been very destructive but there had been no loss of life. The seat of the fire was in a community hall attached to a school and entry had been gained to the premises through the school kitchens, which joined the two buildings and were used by both. Whoever had gone into the hall had used a serving hatch and on the top edge of the glass window was a perfect set of fingerprints. Those fingerprints were my client's. He denied he had ever been in the kitchen. He was lying and the magistrates could have deduced the reason for the lie was to cover his guilt.

He was fifteen years of age and of good character. His parents were clearly caring and supportive – not always the case with juvenile offenders. Because of the seriousness of the fire, I believed a custodial sentence was inevitable, but if he pleaded guilty he might receive a detention centre order rather than be sent to the Crown Court for sentence and the real possibility of being sent for Borstal training. I tried to persuade him that he should admit the offence. He refused. His parents had also tried, as had my instructing solicitor. All to no avail.

I started the trial with a heavy heart, convinced I was just going through the motions, until the prosecuting lawyer called the forensic expert. Usually in cases of arson the expert gives evidence as to the seat of the fire and the method by which it was started. Typically some sort of accelerant is used – petrol, paraffin or alcohol. The expert told the court the fire had started in a plastic ashtray on the bar but did not give evidence of any accelerant being used.

There is a rule of thumb that one never asks a question to which one doesn't know the answer. I decided to take the risk.

'Is it possible the fire started as a result of somebody leaving a lighted cigarette stub in the ashtray?'

'Certainly. If someone had not stubbed out their cigarette properly, the plastic of the ashtray would melt and then ignite.'

The offence of arson requires the prosecution to establish the fire was started deliberately and this they could no longer do. My client was acquitted, and I was relieved my persuasion had failed.

A Date With a Judge

A few years after I had been called to the Bar, I was at a drinks party in The Temple to which a number of judges had been invited. Amongst them was one I knew quite well because he had been a solicitor and appeared at one of the London magistrates' courts on a daily basis. He was about five or six years older than me, single, quite good looking and an entertaining conversationalist, so when he invited me to have dinner with him one evening I accepted. We arranged to meet the following Wednesday outside the Royal Court Theatre in Sloane Square, Chelsea.

On the day of our date, I can't remember what happened but at some time in the afternoon I realised I would be unable to get to Sloane Square by the agreed hour or at all.

This was before the days of mobile phones, so I tried to ring the court where I knew he was sitting. After some delay I was put through to the court clerks' room, only to be told the judge had risen for the day and had left the building. I tried various other numbers, hoping I could catch up with him, but failed to do so. By the time I left court it was so late that I was sure there was no point in even trying to get to Sloane Square. I resolved to write the judge a short note apologising for standing him up, but didn't manage to get round to it as quickly as I should have done.

A couple of days later I was instructed to represent two brothers who were facing various counts of burglary. They both had a number of previous convictions and were reluctant to plead guilty to these new offences, although the evidence against them was fairly conclusive. The case was listed for plea and directions, which meant they would be asked whether they were pleading guilty or not guilty.

I arrived at court determined to persuade them it was in their best interests to plead guilty to the charges on the indictment. Quite often when a defendant pleaded guilty they were sentenced immediately; this was particularly true if they were persistent offenders and the only possible outcome was a custodial sentence. I had anticipated that is what would happen with these two brothers.

When I arrived at the courthouse and checked which judge would be trying the case, my heart sank when I discovered it was the judge I had stood up the previous Wednesday. Here was a dilemma; should I advise them to plead guilty and hope the judge would not inflict any greater sentence because of my actions, or let them plead not guilty and hopefully be in front of a different judge on a later occasion.

I decided my initial opinion was the right one, and in conference with them both I advised them to plead guilty. They were still reluctant and one of them asked me if I knew the judge. I told them I did and that I thought he would be fair and reasonable when he passed sentence on them. I didn't reveal my indiscretion of the previous Wednesday.

They maintained their innocence and I left them in the cells and went up into court, a little relieved that I would not have to mitigate on their behalf in front of a judge I had offended. Just as the two brothers were called into court, the dock officer called to me and said they wanted to speak to me; I had to ask the judge to allow me a few minutes. He did so and when I spoke to my clients they said they had changed their minds and would plead guilty to the indictment.

The judge must have felt he needed to put out of his mind my failure to keep our date, because he said how sensible they had been to accept my advice and gave them what I thought was a very lenient sentence.

The Musician Who Played
With Bob Marley

What happens when one of the jury decides to investigate issues in a trial?

I was defending a man charged with importing cocaine, a Class A drug. The defendant, whose name was Gray, had arrived in the UK from Jamaica via Amsterdam. He was collected by car at Gatwick and driven through the streets of South London towards Brixton. The vehicle was followed by detectives in an unmarked police car. They claimed a package had been thrown from the nearside front window of the car and they had radioed for assistance before stopping the vehicle. The occupants were asked to get out and my client ran off. He didn't get very far before he was arrested and searched. Nothing incriminating was found on him or in the vehicle.

The police searched for the item thrown from the car but couldn't find anything fitting the description or anything that was incriminating. My client disputed he had thrown anything away although he said he might have dropped the packaging from some food out of the passenger window. Not surprisingly the police found plenty of that.

After a thorough search of the area a young police officer found a small parcel containing cocaine in a nearby road. The difficulty for the prosecution was that the package was not found on the route the car had taken, nor close to where my client had run. In his defence I relied on a set of plans of the area and cross-examined the detectives as to which streets the car had been driven along and which ones my client had run along. No police officer was able to say they had seen anything dropped by the defendant as he ran away.

When the officer who had found the package was called he gave the name of the street in which he had found it and he identified the road on the plans. He relied for his evidence on notes he had made as soon as he returned to the police station, as he was entitled to do. I got him to mark the map and asked the jury to do the same on their copies. His explanation for the package not being in the road the defendant had run along was that he must have thrown it over a garden wall.

The next day one of the jurors handed a note for the judge to the usher. He had been to look at the scene and he judged it was impossible to throw anything from one street to the other. The judge was very annoyed because the only evidence a jury can take into account is that which they have heard in court. He had two options. The first was to abort the trial and start again with a different jury; the second was to allow all the jurors the opportunity to look at the location. He chose the latter.

We all had to wait until the afternoon until a coach could be arranged to take the jury and a car to take the judge. Counsel and the police officer had to make their own way. My recollection is that I walked and still arrived before the coach. When the young police officer saw the street he had named, his mouth fell open as he realised he had made a terrible mistake. The judge was furious.

Had the defendant been in possession of the drugs or was it a plant by the police? The jury came to the conclusion they couldn't be sure of the defendant's guilt and acquitted him. I'm sure that police officer would never make the same mistake again.

There was another feature of the case that makes it stick in my memory. Gray was a professional musician and claimed to have played with Bob Marley.

A Day at the Races

I did one other case where the jury were taken for a view of the scene of the crime. The defendants were a couple in their sixties. They were both small, round and grey haired. It would be hard to imagine a more unlikely pair of criminals. They had been charged with handling stolen property – large quantities of cigarettes, hundreds of the sort of packages you can buy duty free. The cigarettes were found in the meat safe of their council flat in North London. They claimed to have no knowledge of them, saying they were hidden there by someone else. They couldn't say who, although the suspicion was that one of their sons was the culprit and he had smuggled them into the country.

At first blush it seemed improbable they were not aware of such a large quantity of cigarettes in their two-bedroomed flat, and that made the location of the meat safe an important issue in the trial. One might have expected the pantry to be in the kitchen but at some stage the flats had been reconfigured and the kitchen moved to the rear. This had resulted in the meat safe being next to the front door. There were photographs of the interior of the flat, which showed the boxes of cigarettes in the meat safe and its location. The couple said they didn't use it and somebody must have placed the packages there when they were in the living room or bedroom. Perhaps if they had been prepared to say the cigarettes had been put there by a member of the family they might have been believed or at least given the benefit of the doubt. Although they would still have been guilty of handling if they agreed to store the goods, but the jury might just have felt sorry for the position they were in and acquitted them.

The trial lasted a couple of days or so and on the Friday I expected the judge to do his summing up and send the jury out, leaving me free to start another case on the following Monday. However, when I arrived at court the usher told me the judge had decided the jury should have the opportunity to see the flat and they were making the necessary arrangements. Eventually we set off in a convoy to the couple's home, a coach for the jury, a large black limousine for the judge, the defendants in a prison van, and I was squashed into a car with the police officer and prosecuting counsel. We got there about lunchtime and everybody was given the opportunity to look round the flat. There wasn't room for us all to get into the property at the same time so we inspected the flat in shifts. When we had finished the judge looked at his watch and said it was too late to go back. He extended my clients' bail.

As the jury were led back to the coach, the limousine took off going north. Back at the Old Bailey, prosecuting counsel and I were discussing whether the 'view' was really necessary when we were interrupted by a more senior member of the Bar. 'Which judge was it?'

We told him, and he then said, 'Is there racing at Newmarket? If there is, he was on his way to the races.'

Chasing Shadows

In 1993, King's Cross in London was well known as a place to buy or sell drugs. In order to clean up the area the police began an operation known as Operation Welwyn. Undercover officers posed as buyers and when they were offered drugs the person selling was arrested and charged with offences under the Misuse of Drugs Act 1971. They used video cameras in fixed positions and also in vans. Many people were arrested in the course of this operation and it resulted in a number of trials. There is a fine line when undercover officers make such a purchase between encouraging the crime and trapping a defendant, which is illegal, and simply taking advantage of the dealer's willingness to supply the drugs.

My client, Angela, was of mixed race and in her mid-twenties. My recollection is she worked in the same area as a prostitute. She was charged with one offence of supplying cocaine in the form of crack. The police officers said they had bought cocaine from her. Angela was filmed meeting the two officers and going to a telephone booth. According to the officers they paid her for drugs and she handed them over when they gave her two twenty-pound notes. That transfer of drugs and money was obscured from the view of the cameras by a large traffic sign pointing the way to Cambridge and The North. There was no question that it was anyone other than the defendant. She was clearly identifiable wearing a denim jacket and her long hair tied up with a brightly coloured ribbon.

Angela was arrested some time later in accordance with a policy adopted by the police to avoid others being alerted to the ongoing operation. When she was interviewed she denied supplying drugs to the police officers but said she made a telephone call to some other person who may have supplied the policewomen with cocaine. If that was the truth then she would still have been guilty of the offence but on a different basis, and that version raised the issue of entrapment. After legal argument before the judge, from which the jury were excluded, prosecuting counsel agreed that the jury could only return a verdict of guilty on the grounds that Angela had personally sold cocaine to the officers.

When the two police officers gave evidence they said they had spoken to Angela on the street and asked her if she had any drugs to sell. She had suggested the deal take place in the telephone booth and they had followed her, but had stood outside while she took the drugs out of her handbag. They had handed her two twenty-pound notes in exchange for the crack. The numbers of the notes had been recorded, but none were found in Angela's possession. The Crown's explanation was she had spent the money between the offence being committed and her arrest.

Although the traffic sign obscured not only the telephone booth but the two officers as well, I could follow their shadows as they crossed the pavement. At no time had they approached the telephone booth; instead, after they had spoken to Angela, they had walked towards a pedestrian crossing where they again became visible on the film. They were unable to explain their movements when I cross-examined them.

The judge trying the case became so interested that on his way home he drove to King's Cross to see for himself the location of the traffic sign and the telephone booth. He told prosecuting counsel and myself that he had done so and asked if either of us had any comment to make. Neither of us did, although my opponent did ask about the jury going to see the location. The judge said that was probably not wise and then summed up for an acquittal. Angela was found not guilty.

The Fortune Teller

The horse fair at Appleby in Cumbria is a well-known meeting place for Romany families, but they also congregate in other places throughout the country. Some of our most famous racecourses are near to sites where Romany families met and showed off their horses and ponies. Many have a continuing interest in horses even if their homes are moved by a different sort of horsepower, and, even if their children don't always go to school, they learn to ride as soon as they can sit on a pony.

One of my cases some years ago was defending a traveller called Smith on a charge of assault occasioning grievous bodily harm and possession of a shotgun without a licence. The incident or should I say series of incidents took place near the coast in East Anglia, which was one of those meeting places like Appleby. By day they raced their horses along the beach and at night blocked off a long stretch of road for trotting competitions.

Horses frequently changed hands at these events, and it was the purchase of a pony for his son that led to the fight for which Smith was now before the court.

He had bought a pony from another traveller who had disguised the animal by painting over its distinguishing features – a white star on its head and four white hocks. When the paint wore off and Smith realised the horse was stolen he demanded his money back. The horse thief refused and threats were exchanged. The abuse mounted until the men had a serious fight in which the thief was given a good hiding by Smith. Matters might have stayed there – Romany families are reluctant to involve the police in their affairs – but Smith was still demanding the return of his money. This time he threatened to use a shotgun on the thief.

The seller of the pony must have taken fright because he called the police anonymously, informing them that Smith had an unlicensed shotgun. The police went to his caravan and spoke to his wife who worked as a fortune teller. Smith in the meantime went missing, taking his guns with him. After a few days he returned home having buried the guns in the sand. When the police came again he denied having any weapons, but it didn't take them long to find the hiding place and Smith was charged with possession of the guns and the earlier assault. He pleaded not guilty to the charges saying the guns were not his, and as for the assault he was acting in self-defence. I think he felt the complainant had only got his just desserts.

The case was tried at Norwich Crown Court, which at that time was in a very old building with no real facilities. I was not optimistic that he would be acquitted; Smith had been a prize fighter at travellers' fairs and the horse thief, for all his dishonesty, looked an unlikely opponent. The guns were identified as having been ones Smith had bought from a licensed dealer only months before. However, the jury went out and to my surprise were still considering their verdict at the lunch adjournment.

The only place to get something to eat was an outdoor café, rather like the ones taxi drivers use. I was standing waiting for my coffee and sandwich with my instructing solicitor, and behind us was prosecuting counsel, when Mrs Smith walked up and asked us how long the jury would be out and what was going to happen. Before I could say anything, counsel for the Crown said,

'Haven't you brought your crystal ball? Then you could tell us.'

The Road Roller

Stag nights can lead to young men doing very silly things. One such party had been held at St Katherine's Dock next to Tower Bridge. As the group left they spotted a road roller parked alongside the pavement. One of their number was familiar with the mechanics of these machines and, after some ribaldry, he accepted a dare to start it. He had moved the vehicle a couple of yards when a police car screeched to a halt beside them. The officer asked them what was going on and one of the group tried to explain. While this conversation was taking place most of the group slipped away, leaving the driver of the road roller and two other young men to face the music.

The policeman wasn't prepared to listen to any explanation and all three were arrested for taking without consent, more usually referred to as TWOC. The three men were placed in the car and taken to Tower Bridge police station. The road roller was potentially an exhibit so one of the officers went to retrieve it and bring it back to the station. He couldn't do so because he didn't know how to start the engine, never mind put it into gear. His solution was to go back and get the man who had been driving it from the cells and get him to bring it across Tower Bridge to the station.

Although TWOC is not the most serious offence in the calendar of crime, because it had taken place in the square mile of the City the trial was listed at the Central Criminal Court, the Old Bailey. They were guilty of the offence, although it was the most theoretical taking without consent one could imagine.

Although it isn't a defence to a charge there is a principle known as *de minimis*, which means if the offence is trivial and taking into account any and all other issues, the Crown should not proceed with the trial as not being in the public interest. I thought this fell into that category.

The outcome of the case was particularly important to one of the three men because he worked for the Ministry of Defence and his superiors took the view that, as it was an offence of dishonesty, he would be sacked if he was convicted. Counsel for the other two defendants and I spoke to the prosecuting barrister and tried to persuade her to drop the case, but she refused. She insisted it was a serious case.

'Well, it did take place outside the Tower. Could have been treason,' one of my colleagues said.

Fortunately, the judge was of the same view as the other defending counsel and me, and suggested to the prosecution they may want to consider their position and not waste the court's time on such a trivial matter. The prosecution saw sense and the case was dropped. The young men got a telling off from the judge and they all kept their jobs.

The Unquiet American

In the calendar of offences, threatening behaviour comes fairly near the bottom, although it can have disastrous consequences. It is an offence for which there is no right of election to have the case tried by a jury, so senior barristers are only rarely instructed in such cases. However, I was instructed to represent a defendant who had been convicted of threatening behaviour and a common assault in the magistrates' court and was appealing that decision to the Crown Court. The appeal would be heard by a judge and two magistrates, but no jury.

The defendant was an American and was in his late forties. I can't remember his name so I'll call him Walt. The circumstances of the case did have an unusual twist. Walt had gone to buy fish and chips at a shop near to his home. He had gone on his bicycle intending to return with the meal for him and his girlfriend. When he arrived at the shop he propped the bike up against the plate-glass window. As he joined the queue, Mike, one of the grown-up sons of the owner, who was serving in the shop, asked him to move the bicycle. Walt began to argue with Mike and the language became more abusive. The shouting match escalated when Walt said Mike's brother, who had been murdered about eighteen months previously, had probably deserved it.

Mike grabbed hold of the bike and threw it into the road, damaging the front wheel. Walt was very angry and a scuffle started. The police were called and Walt was arrested. At the police station Walt was interviewed under caution by a female detective sergeant. He said she was rude and that she refused to listen to his account of the evening's events and told him the damage to his cycle was minimal; she said had no intention of arresting Mike for an offence of criminal damage, nor for any assault on Walt.

It transpired later she had been involved in the investigation of the murder of Mike's brother and at one stage had been the family liaison officer. Walt's view was that she was a biased investigator in his case and she could not envisage the shop owners and their family could lie. He may have been right.

Unusually the local police station had conducted the murder inquiry rather than the Murder Squad. I assumed it was because the murderer was known and had recently been released from a secure hospital in the area.

As a way of proving the police were not independent of the fish shop owner's family, Walt decided to keep watch on the premises and count the number of times officers arrived and, he said, were given food. There were further incidents but none serious. No one was arrested but Walt was warned not to persist in his surveillance. He didn't take any notice of the warning and continued, often in disguise. He didn't fool anyone and in the end an injunction was obtained to keep him away from the shop.

When the case came to trial in the magistrates' court, Walt was convicted. The evidence he had put together alleging police bias was disallowed. He decided to appeal and it was then I was instructed to represent him in the Crown Court.

Walt was an interesting character, half American and half German. He had two older sisters; all were the result of the relationship between an American soldier stationed in Germany and a local woman. Walt told me the United States Army were against marriages between natives and members of the armed forces. Nor were they interested in assisting immigration by families the soldiers had established in Germany. His father was sent back to the USA leaving his mother to bring up the three children alone in a war-torn country.

His father kept in touch with the family but after a few years he wrote to say he had married an American woman (shades of Pinkerton), and he wanted the children to come and live with him so they could have a better life. Walt's mother reluctantly agreed. The two girls went first and he joined them when he was seven.

To his horror he found himself taken to a wooden shack in the backwoods of Mississippi, where he and his sisters were treated as little more than slaves. Their father's wife, instead of being a mother to them, forced them to do a lot of the housework. There was no electricity, no running water, and Walt's job was to chop what seemed an endless supply of timber. They were forbidden to speak German together and were beaten when they did. Nor were they sent to school.

One day, when he was about nine years old, Walt decided to run away. He was fortunate in making it to the high road where he was picked up by the local sheriff. The equivalent of our local authority was informed. The two girls were found and all three were placed in the care of the local authority. However, the three siblings could not be kept together and they were adopted by different families. Walt ended up in Florida with a quite wealthy couple who had no children. They encouraged him to speak German and he went on to university. When they died he inherited their wealth. He said there was not an enormous amount but enough for him to come and live in the UK without having to find work, and to buy a modest flat in London. He described himself as a writer and poet.

He began a search for his mother and his sisters and was able to locate his mother before she died. His father he never wanted to see again. Just before the incident he had found his sisters; they had an emotional reunion in the States with the sheriff who rescued them.

The trial in the Crown Court took four days. We had sought discovery and had obtained the papers about the murder investigation, which illustrated how close local police officers had become to the family. The judge, probably on the basis that it could do no harm, let the evidence about that relationship be given to the court. Similarly, I was allowed to ask the sergeant about her connection with the family and about her bias in favour of the fish shop owner.

Walt gave evidence and admitted the threatening words in the witness box, but he was acquitted of the common assault charge. He wasn't happy about the conviction. I advised him he had no grounds to take the matter to the Court of Appeal and I thought he had accepted that.

Then I received a number of letters from him asking to see the notes I had taken at the hearing and a copy of my closing speech. I declined and he reported me to the Bar Council – something every barrister dreads. When I explained the reasons for not letting him have my notes the Bar Council dismissed his complaint. Anyway, my writing was so bad I couldn't read the notes of my speech myself, so I doubt they would have given him any assistance.

The Lemsip Rapists

Sometimes the defendants, the scene and the facts of a case can seem so bizarre that no writer could ever invent such a story. The pair described in the press as the Lemsip Rapists were just such characters. The two men were an unlikely pair, one of Middle Eastern extraction, aged about fifty, and the other a thirty-something Londoner who had made good. The scene of the rape was a top-floor suite in a Park Lane hotel. The suite comprised two bedrooms, each with its own bathroom, a sitting room and a dining room, which was furnished as an office. The elder of the two was an arms dealer who, when he was in London, lived and worked from this suite of rooms. He wasn't my client so I was never privy to the ins and outs of his business.

My client was the younger man who was employed to run the office and ensure all the paperwork for exporting weapons was in order.

Most of the work they did seemed to involve meetings with clients, discussing their requirements, which seemed to range from handguns to helicopters, arranging the purchase and, most importantly, end-user certificates. I wasn't in any doubt that most of the transactions were illegal.

The young woman who alleged rape was another employee. She was a temporary secretary who was recruited through an employment agency. It was quite a nice job. Her hours were flexible and lunch, as well as tea and coffee, was available from room service.

On the day in question she had come into work with a very heavy cold. During the course of the morning the older man prepared a glass of Lemsip for her and told her to go and lie down in one of the bedrooms. Her case was that he had put some drugs into the drink that made her very drowsy and she had passed out in the bedroom, only coming to when he was on top of her and having sexual intercourse with her. Further, she said, when he had finished my client had come into the bedroom and also had intercourse with her against her will. Both men denied the allegations but when interviewed by the police they told very different stories from each other – stories that were mutually incompatible.

The older man said the woman had made the allegation up and she was trying to blackmail him in respect of some of the arms deals he had made. My client said his employer had raped the girl and she had sought solace in his arms and that had resulted in them having intercourse. It was an almost hopeless case to defend; not only was there a conflict between the two defendants but a forensic examination of the hotel suite found traces of a white powder: crushed sleeping tablets. Both men denied having brought any drugs into the hotel, but of course the rooms had been used by a number of guests in the preceding weeks. They argued the insides of wardrobes and cupboards were not always swept clean.

At the start of the trial, the QC representing the older man and the QC leading me for the younger one made applications to sever the trial. The judge was not having that. In some ways it was less of a disadvantage to us than it was for the co-defendant, because if his counter-allegation of blackmail succeeded it was unlikely the jury would convict our client.

What emerged during the trial was that the young woman had gone home and told her family what had happened. Her father and brother had then gone to the hotel and confronted the two men, threatened them and demanded a very large sum of money, my recollection is something in the region of twenty-five thousand pounds, with the promise the allegation of rape would not be reported to the police. The family members just happened to all have criminal convictions for armed robberies and a previous for extortion, which lent some credibility to the older man's story.

Some payment was made and again the defence for the older man could prove that a large sum of money had been drawn from his account and on the same day the woman's relations had visited the hotel and gone up to the suite. The receptionist confirmed a couple of men had come to the hotel and asked for the older man; telephone records of calls from the reception desk to the suite were consistent with the visit.

The older man also said he told the girl's family he needed time to raise the rest of the cash. The allegation of rape was not made to the police for a few days which supported that From the prosecution point of view it meant that there was no forensic medical evidence to support the allegation, and from the defence they could argue the delay was to see if the girl's family would get the rest of the money they had demanded. Instead of trying to raise the extra sum the older defendant left the hotel and was arrested at Heathrow on his way back to the Middle East. My client had no such opportunity to escape and was arrested the next day. During interviews the older man denied the offence but chose not to reply to any further questions he was asked by the investigating officers. My client would have done better to do the same, but he chose to answer, insisting the sexual intercourse was consensual.

The trial lurched from problem to problem as the evidence was given before the jury. The young woman maintained they had both raped her. Her father and brother both said they had been to see the two men – they said with the intention of a revenge attack but then thought better of it. The older man's reluctance to say anything about his unsavoury business didn't help anyone. The two defence Silks were continually arguing and attacking each other, which allowed the female Silk prosecuting to have a field day. The favourite phrase was 'It's like trying to fight with one hand tied behind your back.' Not surprisingly both men were convicted and were sentenced to seven years' imprisonment.

Did the court hear the truth and nothing but the truth? I don't think they did. I believe

there was more to this than any of the parties
were prepared to admit.

Night Epilepsy

One of the best jury advocates I worked with was Victor Durand, a small man with a huge egg-shaped bald head, bags under his eyes and a large nose. He was about seventy when he led me in a very unusual murder case.

Our client, Danny, a man in his late twenties, lived in a council flat in North London with his girlfriend. On the night of the incident, he had been drinking with his friend, John, in a local pub. Towards the end of the evening they argued and, as the disagreement became more heated, Danny left the pub and stormed off home. He suffered from a type of epilepsy that only occurred at night. In order to minimise the risk of an epileptic fit that was potentially life threatening, he took various drugs just before he went to bed. He did so on this night.

He and his girlfriend had just gone to sleep when they were awoken by a banging at the front door. The flat was on the third floor of the block and access was by an external staircase onto a terrace. Danny went to the front door and opened it. The first thing he saw was a carving knife waving in his face. The knife was being wielded by John, who was shouting and swearing at Danny.

Danny believed he was being threatened and, he said, feared for his life. He ran to the kitchen and picked up a chopping knife, ran back to the door and stabbed John. His girlfriend had already phoned the police. They arrived shortly after and found John lying on his back bleeding profusely. They attempted resuscitation on him but to no avail.

Danny was arrested and taken to the police station. It was quite late at night by this time and the prescribed drugs he had taken had taken effect. A doctor was called who advised he be allowed to sleep before he was questioned.

The next morning he was interviewed under caution and gave the account I have described. The detectives interviewing accused him of lying because the scene had been searched and no knife had been found apart from the one Danny had used. He was charged with murder and remanded in custody.

When the forensic pathologist carried out the post mortem and turned the body to remove the clothing he found a knife tucked into the waistband of John's trousers, which confirmed, at least in part, Danny's account of the incident.

The question of whether he was guilty of murder or not raised the issue of self-defence. He insisted he was defending himself and that John was threatening him with the knife.

Self-defence is not always easy to establish, particularly when someone has died. When the judge directs the jury he tells them, 'It is good law and good sense that a man may defend himself. It is both good law and good sense that a man may do, but only do, what is necessary and reasonable. You need to ask if the force was necessary to deal with the threat the defendant faced. If the use of force was necessary, did the defendant use only reasonable force, taking into consideration the circumstances in which he found himself? A man is not expected to judge to a nicety the exact degree of force to use.'

At the time Danny stabbed his friend, John did not have the knife in his hands and was outside the flat. The prosecution argued Danny should not have armed himself, but should have closed the door and waited for the police to arrive. So the question was whether Danny had acted reasonably. There is a further element to the issue of reasonableness because the jury has to take into account the peculiarities of the defendant. They must ask themselves if a man with these characteristics acted reasonably. At the time of the incident, Danny was under the influence of his prescribed medication and we were able to call an eminent psychiatrist who told the court the effect of the drugs would be to lower his ability to assess the threat he faced.

Victor Durand addressed the jury with great skill, holding the two knives side by side to demonstrate the difference in their sizes, the one John had waved being much bigger than the one Danny had used. He was found not guilty.

Victor asked for Danny to be discharged and the judge granted that application. Despite the verdict and the judge ordering his discharge, Danny was returned to the cells for his property to be restored to him. I started to walk the short distance to the lift which would take me down to the custody area, as most defence counsel do, hoping to be thanked. Victor refused to accompany me and walked away muttering that Danny was clearly guilty.

Sisters in Crime

The *modus operandi*, usually abbreviated to MO, of the five Gordon sisters relied on the similarity in their appearance, despite the age range from seventeen to thirty-two. They were of similar height and their hair was cut to the same length, almost grazing their shoulders, and was a dark blonde with silvery highlights. They were similarly proportioned, neither too overweight nor too slim, unless they were pregnant, and they wore almost identical clothes. They all had at least one small child, and two of the children were mixed race, but they too would be dressed in very similar clothing. The family acted like a pack of lionesses looking after each other's children.

The sisters would go into various shops – Marks and Spencer was their favourite – usually in a group, and then split up as they wandered around looking at clothes. Some of the items were then secreted in the back of the pushchairs. The one who had taken the clothes would then switch her pram containing her own child to another of the sisters and take that one's child.

Normally the store detectives would wait until the sister they thought they had seen taking something from the display gondolas and hide it was outside the store. But by that time she no longer had the stolen items and could look aghast at being stopped and accused of theft. Sometimes they were caught, but never all of them.

That was until CCTV.

Eventually the Gordon sisters were arrested as a result of cameras recording their activities in the shopping mall in Milton

Keynes. The video showed the sisters outside Marks and Spencer transferring items of clothing from one to another. An inspector purported to identify the sisters and accordingly they were charged with conspiracy to steal. In addition, various members of the family faced a number of charges of theft. The trial was listed in front of Judge Slack at Aylesbury Crown Court. I was instructed to represent the eldest of the sisters, Martha.

Just before the trial was due to start an usher told me the judge wanted to see me in his chambers. He told me that if they all pleaded guilty he was mindful of their family responsibilities and he would not prevent them from looking after their children. I went back to the robing room and told co-defending counsel of the judge's indication on sentence. It took a bit of effort to persuade all the girls to plead guilty to enough of the charges to satisfy the prosecution, but in the end they agreed. Judge Slack kept his promise and they were all given suspended sentences and a stiff warning about the consequences if they continued their activities.

Later the judge told me that he wanted them to plead guilty because he knew he would not be able to avoid laughing when I cross-examined the officer, as he knew I would, about the officer's ability to identify the sisters. He claimed he could tell which sister was which from their legs.

The sisters, however, did not heed Judge Slack's warning.

Some months later they were arrested again. This time the store detectives together with the police employed different tactics. The sisters and their mother had, once again, gone to Milton Keynes to steal from Marks and Spencer in the shopping centre. When they arrived on the outskirts of the city they parked their two vehicles, leaving Mum to look after the cars and some of the younger children. Once inside the shopping mall they were kept under observation by a team of store detectives, who watched as they stole over twenty items from their favourite store. This time, instead of arresting the sisters as soon as they left, they were followed back to their cars, and, as they unloaded the stolen items of clothing into the boot, they were all arrested by police officers, including Mrs Gordon.

The case was committed for trial at Luton Crown Court on a charge of conspiracy to steal. The indictment also had a number of charges of theft and it was to those they pleaded guilty. They had no alternative. They were not so fortunate in the judge this time. My recollection is that he called them a scourge on the country, a gang of modern-day poachers. All of them were given custodial sentences, including their mother, despite her having no convictions for many years. The sentences for the sisters varied depending on their previous convictions, the youngest getting the least, but that earlier suspended sentence was imposed consecutively on all five.

That evening fourteen children were taken into care in the absence of anyone to look after them.

Never Call Mother

Identification issues used to be a frequent problem for the courts. The case of George Davies highlighted how unreliable an eyewitness can be. As an aside, a friend of mine was involved with the *Free George Davies* campaign and was one of those who dug up the cricket pitch at Headingley just before a test match.

In my case, a twenty-three-year-old had been charged with armed robbery of a building society in the East End of London. The allegation was that he had gone into the banking hall with a sawn-off shotgun and threatened the cashier to hand over the money in her till. The premises had video surveillance and the Crown were relying on the video of the scene to identify my client, who had denied being the culprit and claimed he was at home in South London at the time of the offence.

There was no other evidence. The cashier couldn't identify him, nor could any of the other customers in the office at the time. There were no fingerprints or DNA at the scene to link my client to the crime. After his arrest he was interviewed, and he provided and alibi claiming he was at home with his sister and his mother. When a suspect provides an alibi, the defence must serve a formal notice on the prosecution giving the details of where the defendant was at the relevant time and the witnesses he will call to support it. The prosecution then take statements from those witnesses in the hope of undermining them. This they had done unsuccessfully in this case. I had no reason to doubt the defendant's mother and sister would be good witnesses.

The video was sometimes out of focus. At other times, there was only a partial view or one that was obscured by Christmas decorations. There was one good shot of the robber's face – as he turned away from the counter and walked towards the door he had looked up directly into the camera. I played the video many times, trying to decide if the man shown was my client. I wasn't sure and, of course, the jury in order to convict must be.

The trial at the Old Bailey went well. I could see the jury were doubtful the man on the video and the defendant were the same person. I called my client to give evidence. Despite the most rigorous cross-examination he maintained he had been at home on the evening of the offence. It was Christmas Eve and he had watched the television with his sister and mother. He gave an account of the programmes they had seen. His sister confirmed his story and she too was a compelling witness. I began to think I would win the case and my client would be acquitted.

Then I called the second alibi witness, his mother, and as she walked into the court I knew the case was over. Her face showed the same characteristics as the face on the video. The robber could only have been her son.

As Sober as a Judge

We like to think that our judges are, well, just and are, at least when on the bench, upright, sober men and women. The majority are but just occasionally they misbehave and the mask of respectability slips.

One day I was representing a woman, let's call her Muriel, charged with obtaining social security by fraudulently claiming benefits to which she was not entitled. As usual she was a single mum trying to support her family with too little money. I can't now remember the exact nature of the lie she had told to increase the welfare payments, but it was probably the small amount she earned from working part time. It wasn't the first time Muriel had been before the courts for similar offences although it was some years since the last conviction.

She pleaded guilty to three offences of obtaining benefit by fraud and I said what I could on her behalf. My plea in mitigation fell on deaf ears and she was sentenced to six months on each count.

My recollection is that I had other cases at court that day, so I was still in the building in the late afternoon, when I was asked to go to the cells. Once down in the bowels of the courthouse I was told by one of the prison officers that the judge had requested my client be taken back up to the dock. I went to see her in her cell. She was a small woman, dark eyes now red-rimmed, and dark brown hair scraped back into a ponytail. She wanted to know why the judge wanted to see her again. I told her I didn't know.

After my brief conversation with her I went back into the courtroom. None of the lights in the room were on; high windows let in a dim grey light. The panelling around the walls, the judge's bench and all the seating were dark wood, making it seem more sombre and more austere. The judge's bench was raised up and stretched across the width of the room. To one side of the raised area was a red curtain hanging from a heavy brass pole. Behind the curtain was the door to the judge's chambers.

I was the only person in the room; there were no ushers and no clerk. After a few minutes Muriel was brought into the high dock at the rear by two prison officers. We all waited in silence.

Suddenly the curtain was swept aside and the judge staggered onto the bench. He wasn't wearing his wig or his gown. Lawyers' tabs round the wing collar of his white shirt were the only remaining part of his court dress. In his right hand he had a half-full wine glass that he was waving around. He took three steps into the room, turned to look at Muriel and said, 'Those sentences, they're consecutive not concurrent.' Having said that he turned slightly, raised the wine glass, said 'Cheers' and drained it before fumbling his way back into his chambers.

The sentences being consecutive meant a term of eighteen months imprisonment, not six. Fortunately the prison officers ignored the impromptu and probably illegal sentencing session and recorded the sentence as concurrent.

There must have been a fair number of social security frauds when I was in practice, because another incident with a judge behaving badly also concerned a woman who had obtained welfare payments by deception. My own opinion was that too many judges had no idea how difficult it was to manage on so little money. Most lawyers would have thought nothing of paying forty pounds for a pair of children's shoes – it was less than they would spend on a bottle of wine. But the law is the law and it is taxpayer's money.

The woman I was instructed to represent had also been charged with the offences of obtaining welfare payments by deception. It wasn't her first court appearance and she had previously been given a suspended prison sentence to enable her to see a psychologist in the hope that dealing with some of her many problems would stop her reoffending. It had not and although the probation officer was asking for another chance – she had failed to keep the appointments with the psychologist on occasions for perfectly proper reasons – I thought she was likely to go to prison. No one should forget that sending a woman to prison often means that children have to go into care.

Despite my own opinion I stood up to mitigate and ask the judge to consider taking the course that the probation officer suggested, which I think was a further period on probation. The judge was not having it and kept interrupting me. I persisted in mitigating on behalf of my client in accordance with my instructions, at which point the judge began to yell at me.

'Miss Barnes, will you sit down and be quiet.'

'With respect, Your Honour,' a respect I was not feeling at that precise moment, 'if I can just finish …'

'No, you cannot,' he said.

'But, Your Honour …' I was interrupted again.

'Sit down. Sit down.' By this time the judge was purple in the face and looked like he was bursting at the seams. I expected his wig to begin bouncing on his head.

At first I didn't sit down, because I thought he would see he was being unreasonable and hear me out, and then impose whatever custodial sentence he thought appropriate. Instead he roared at me to sit down. This time I complied. He stormed off the bench, leaving me in the courtroom. The ushers, clerk, prison staff and warrant officer were all open-mouthed at his behaviour.

He sent a message that the case was to be transferred to another court where the judge who had imposed the suspended sentence was sitting – and he did treat her with some leniency and made the Probation Order.

That episode with such a difficult judge contributed, I believe, to the decision by the Lord Chancellor's Office to refuse my application for Silk. It wasn't the events in court but my reaction to them, which meant I was thought to be 'not quite the right style for Silk.'

The judge's behaviour towards me in the course of that hearing left me feeling rather bruised. In my view I had been belittled in court in front of my client, other barristers, solicitors and probation staff. Many of the court staff were shocked by his behaviour and had apologised as if it was their fault.

I heard nothing from the judge until a couple of weeks later I was at the same court and one of the court clerks said the judge would like to see me in chambers. I asked if prosecuting counsel in my case was wanted as well.

'No. He's just asked for you. I think it's about the other week.'

We both knew what she meant. I didn't want to go and see him at 10 a.m. before court sat, not least because he liked to offer a glass of sherry to counsel invited to his chambers and I refused to drink at that time in the morning. On other occasions I had poured mine into the soil surrounding a potted plant, but on my own I would find that impossible. But, and more importantly to me, his rude remarks had taken place in open court; I felt he should make his apology in court as well. I knew it was never going to happen. I declined his invitation and, although there was never a repetition of that scene, nevertheless I had clearly been struck off his Christmas card list (not that I was ever on it) and I suspect was deemed by him to be unsuitable for Silk.

A Rejected Child

Most of the cases of incest we hear about are fathers and daughters, but the offence covers other relationships where there is consanguinity. Very often those cases involving a brother and sister are not prosecuted if the parties concerned are both consenting adults, but in the case I am about to describe, the sister was underage and her mother was on the warpath.

The defendant David X was in his early twenties and his story was unusual and, I found, rather upsetting. He was the younger of two brothers; their mother had died when he was three and his brother five. They remained living with their father and, when he remarried only a couple of years later, his new wife took on the role of their mother. For two years all was fine, but then problems began to arise that were no fault of the two boys, now aged seven and nine.

The wife was Australian and her mother became ill back in that country. Trying to organise care for her mother at that distance was difficult, and then the stepmother suffered a miscarriage. Not surprisingly she was very upset and she blamed the loss of her baby on the stress of having the responsibility of caring for two boisterous young boys. What happened between the boys' father and her was never disclosed but it resulted in the brothers being put into the care of the local authority with a view to adoption. The boys were separated and went to live with different families. Their stepmother then became pregnant and gave birth to a baby girl.

When the elder brother was twenty-one he decided he wanted to find his birth parents. His search took a little time but eventually he was able to meet his father, stepmother and half-sister. They were welcoming and he liked them. David was reluctant to meet them; he said he felt uneasy about having contact with the woman he considered to have abandoned them. After a few months he was persuaded to go with his elder brother to their home. Although he was distant with his stepmother, he had an immediate rapport with his sister, and they soon established a close relationship.

David was an industrious young man and had saved almost enough money for the deposit for a one-bedroomed flat. (This was some years ago when property in London was more affordable.) His father agreed to provide some extra money and assist David with obtaining a mortgage.

After David moved into the flat, his half-sister became a frequent visitor. She was fifteen and what had been a close friendship quickly developed into a real attachment and eventually they became romantically involved. The relationship didn't last for long; the girl's mother found out about it and it was she who reported it to the police. The girl was reluctant to give a statement but under some pressure from her mother she did do so. David denied the offence when he was interviewed.

The trial took place at the Old Bailey in front of a judge who might have come straight out of central casting; I don't know if he was an Old Etonian, but he had certainly been to public school. I thought he was a good judge for this case; I knew him to be fairly independent-minded and I thought likely to be lenient. I tried to persuade David to plead guilty to the offence but he continued to deny he had had sexual intercourse with his sister.

As I had warned him, his sister although reluctant was a compelling witness; she did not want to condemn her brother and was desperate for him not to be punished. She was adamant that she had not been forced into having intercourse and said she loved him.

David's case was that although there had been some physical relationship it had fallen short of sexual intercourse and his sister had made that up at the instigation of her mother. She was such an obviously truthful witness that cross-examination was difficult. Despite, I thought, some quite skilful cross-examination by me, she repeated the assertion that they had sexual intercourse and denied her mother had suggested she say they had when they had not. However, her mother did not present in the same way. There was no suggestion of any reluctance to give evidence against her stepson – she spoke in anger rather than in sorrow. Her reasons for abandoning the two little boys seemed feeble when she tried to explain in the cold light of the courtroom, yet there was no hint of remorse about it; her own interests were paramount.

When David's father gave evidence, he told the court how guilty he felt when his new wife had said she could no longer care for his sons. He had tried to find ways for them to stay together but in the end it proved impossible.

'I have felt guilty about it every day since. I was so glad when they came to find me and to see how well they had been brought up.' He went on to say that he had not thought through how difficult the reconciliation might be between the two families.

David gave evidence and the jury heard how he had felt, first at the loss of his mother, and then how happy he had been when his father remarried because he had a mother again. He explained that his stepmother had been kind and loving towards him and his elder brother and he had believed they would live happily as a family forever. He described going with his father to some offices – at the time he didn't know what they were – and being left there with his elder brother. At first he thought his father and mother would come back for him, but soon he realised they would not. Although he and his brother were sent to different foster parents and then adopted by different families, he felt he had been lucky with his adoptive parents who he described as being loving and supportive. Certainly one or other of them came to court each day.

When it came to describing the reunion with his father and stepmother, he said he felt uneasy, particularly with his stepmother. He acknowledged they had helped him to buy his flat and furnish it. He had been thrilled to find he had a sister and, he said, the two of them had a similar sense of humour, enjoyed the same music and liked similar food. When he moved into his flat, she began to visit him after school and in the evenings. At first they had just played music but then they had begun to kiss and cuddle each other. He felt flattered by her attention and although he knew he should not encourage her he didn't stop her from visiting him, but he did not have intercourse with her. He asserted that it was his stepmother, who he believed hated him, who had persuaded his sister to make the allegations against him.

The jury listened carefully to his account. Certainly when I was addressing them, concentrating as I did on the stepmother's attitude, some of the jurors nodded sympathetically and one or two of the women wiped what appeared to be tears from their eyes, but in light of the sister's evidence David was convicted.

In my plea in mitigation I stressed how David and his sister had not grown up in the same family and so the usual relationship between brother and sister had not developed. I asked the judge to take into account the loss of his birth mother and then the abandonment by his father and the stepmother he had learnt to trust. In passing sentence the judge said that David may have been abandoned at seven, but his father and stepmother had made it up to him by helping him with the purchase of his flat. Surely, I thought, only someone who had been sent to a prep school at a similar young age could think money could make up for the trauma the seven-year-old child had suffered. However, he passed a very lenient sentence on David – I think a short period of community service, so perhaps the sentence reflected what he thought was required by the system and in his

heart he was a seven-year-old sent away to
school.

Desperate Wives

Early in my career I did work in the family court and one Friday afternoon I had strange experience. The court was very busy so that even after lunch the waiting hall was heaving. There were young men waiting to be called: some alone, others in groups or with teenage girls clinging to them. Dark-suited solicitors carrying large files moved amongst the crowd marshalling their clients, and bewigged barristers tried to take last-minute instructions above the chatter and the sound of shuffling feet.

I threaded my way through the clusters of people until I found my client, Sharon Hurst, a young-looking nineteen-year-old with long wispy blonde hair. There were three women with her who, I learnt, were from the Battered

Wives Refuge in this coastal town. I needed to go through my instructions with Sharon, so we went to look for an empty interview room, leaving the others behind in the hall.

It was one of those dark grey December days and the interview rooms looked worse than usual. I didn't like them; everyone passing from the offices and the robing room could see who was in them and although they could not hear anything, the body language was sufficient to give those passing a hint of how well, or otherwise, a conference was proceeding. This one was not going well at all. Sharon was reluctant to confirm the events described in her affidavit. I persisted, questioning her about the allegation that her boyfriend, Colin Fenton, had been waiting for her near to the Refuge, and had followed her back there every day for the last week.

'You say here that he took your baby, Angelina, and ran off with her? You followed but couldn't keep up so you went round to the flat you had shared with him?'

'Yes. I didn't know what else to do.'

'You went into the flat to get Angelina, but when you tried to leave he locked the door and you couldn't get out?'

'That's right. I hadn't any keys to the flat in my purse.'

'How did you get out?'

'He let me out.'

'Just like that?'

'Well, he'd gone on about me coming back so when I said I'd think about it, but I needed a day or two, he let me go.'

'Anything else happen while you were there?'

Sharon looked away, trying to find something else to focus on so she didn't have to look at me. Eventually she replied, 'What you suggesting?'

'I'm not suggesting anything, but you will be asked questions by Colin's barrister about what happened at your flat.'

There was a pause. Sharon chewed on her lower lip and then said, 'Nothing happened. Just an argument 'bout me going back.'

I wasn't sure she was telling the truth, but I couldn't take it any further without calling her a liar, so I finished the interview by explaining we would have to wait most of the afternoon before we were called into court. Sharon went to get her three companions and they all returned to the interview room. They were anxious to give her advice and they were all smoking heavily, so I moved to a corner of the room to work on the brief.

As the afternoon wore on and work ceased in all but the closed family court, the place became silent. Daylight faded and, because nobody turned the light on in the room, the five of us were left waiting in the dim light to be called into court.

The conversation of the four women became intermittent and finally ceased. The silence was almost tangible. One of the women was about the same age as I was, certainly in her thirties. She was dressed in a style I liked, not least because it was so different from the black suits I was compelled to wear. She looked rather artistic, as if she might be a potter or something similar. Her blue coat was hip length and underneath she wore a floral-print skirt, and a white scarf was twisted round her neck. Her hair was a mass of dark curls that looked as if they needed combing and her face was small with large dark eyes. On the ring finger of her left hand, instead of a wedding band, she wore a ring with a large green pebble-shaped stone.

This woman began to talk in a low voice. There was an urgency in the tone that made me want to listen. 'The doctor gave me antidepressants after I had each of the kids. I had this postnatal depression. You know what it's like?' She paused and looked round at the others but there was no response to her question, so she continued.

'Mind you, it wasn't really the babies that were the problem. It was him. He was always more violent just after the children were born. He'd wait 'til I was breastfeeding and then start to hit me round my head. I couldn't do nothing. Well, you can't do much holding a baby in your arms, can you?'

She didn't pause for an answer but went on, 'I'd just curl up over the little 'un to protect him from his dad. The other two would be crying and pulling at him to try and stop him. But it made no difference – he'd just push them away.

'One year, it was the year Eddie was born, it was coming up to Christmas and I thought

I've had enough. What I need is a nice quiet Christmas. So what did I do?'

She sat back, took a small, battered tin from her pocket, opened it, used the contents to prepare a thin cigarette which she lit and then inhaled deeply.

'What did I do? Christmas Eve I got my pills and crushed them into his beer. Well, he was too drunk to notice. That'll keep him quiet, I thought. He'll have such a headache tomorrow he won't want to get up and me and the kids can enjoy ourselves without him.'

She was tapping her left hand gently, but persistently, on the tabletop. 'I thought he was about to go to sleep in the chair so I got him upstairs, got his clothes off and rolled him into bed. Well, it was quiet. He slept all Christmas Day and Boxing Day as well. I thought I'd killed him.'

She took a quick intake of breath, put her cupped hand to her mouth and whispered, 'Course, sometimes, I almost wish I had.

'I kept going upstairs to see if he was still breathing. Eventually he came to. He couldn't believe he'd slept through Christmas Day and Boxing Day. He went on at me until I told him what I'd done. I got a real pasting. He threatened to go to the police about it but he didn't. For a while he laid off me, but then he started again. That's it, I thought, I'm leaving.'

The youngest shifted uneasily in her seat; she was a thin, pale woman in her twenties, her long face emphasised by her shoulder length light brown hair. Her thin white blouse, partly unbuttoned revealing a gold necklace, was tucked into the waistband of a short denim skirt. She had taken off her leather bomber jacket and hung it over the back of her chair even though it was quite chilly.

The threat to make a complaint to the police by her friend's husband must have struck a chord with the young woman.

'Mine did go to the police but they didn't believe him. They told him he must have fallen down drunk and that's how he'd got the cut on his head. I did laugh about it later but …' She looked down and took a deep breath. 'Well, he's a big lad. They just couldn't believe I could hit him that hard.' She turned to the older woman. 'He is a big bloke, isn't he?' she asked.

'Yes. You only come up to his armpit. I'm not surprised the police didn't believe him.'

'Course he was drunk. He'd gone up town to watch Arsenal – been drinking all day leaving me with the kids. He'd promised to come home straight after the match so I could go to bingo with me mum. When he came in he was plastered, wanting his tea. I had a go at him and told him to make his own. He still had his silly supporter's hat on, a bowler painted in red-and-white stripes. He was sat there yelling about his tea, telling me what he wouldn't do to me if I didn't get him some food.'

The young woman continued, 'So I picked up the poker and hit him over the head with it from behind. Once I started I just kept hitting until his hat lifted up from his head, sort of popped up, and the blood poured down his face in little streams. He looked at me, his eyes wide open, put his hands up to his face, touching it.'

She demonstrated, putting her hands to her forehead and then her cheeks. 'I think he thought I'd poured something over his head. When he looked at his hands and saw that it was blood he made a dive for me but I got out of the way and he fell on the floor. The hat came off and there was blood everywhere.

'I didn't know if it was the booze or me hitting him that made him fall over, but I didn't wait to find out. I grabbed the kids and ran to my mum's. I wasn't dressed properly, still had me slippers on. I didn't dare go back. So, I stayed there and the police came looking for me. They said they'd found him in the street, drunk, with this nasty cut to his head and he'd told them I'd done it.

'"Don't be silly," I said. "Look at me. I'm only half his size."

'"Well, do you want to go and see him?" they said. "We'll take you up there if you want."

'"No, I think I'll wait 'til he's sobered up a bit."

'"Might be best," they said.'

The young woman who had been speaking put her hands to her face, covering her eyes, bent her head down towards the table, pushed her fingers through her hair, pulling it back from her face, and then looked round at the others and smiled tentatively at them. 'I haven't been back.'

I didn't know what to think. Had both women been telling the truth? Weren't they the victims of violence, not the perpetrators?

Sharon turned in her seat towards me. She appeared to be surprised that I was still there but asked when they would be going into court. I said I didn't know but the usher would call us. Sharon sighed and turned back to face her friends. The eldest of the three women reached over and patted Sharon's hand. I had hardly noticed her before but now as she tried to comfort Sharon I realised not only was she older than the others but she was dressed in more expensive clothes. Her white mac was belted and she wore a blue silk scarf tightly knotted; both had seen better days.

Her brown hair, which she wore in an untidy French pleat, was beginning to go grey and the lenses of her gold-rimmed glasses were thick, emphasising her brown eyes.

The room was completely dark; the only light was from the street lamps and the lighting in the corridor. A telephone rang somewhere in the building and there was a squeal of brakes from outside. The familiar noises, breaking the silence, acted as a stimulus and conversation was resumed. They talked about the hostel and how difficult it was living with a number of other women and children. They spoke of those who let their kids run riot, who didn't do their share of cleaning the bathrooms and kitchen, who took other people's food from the fridge and who always got their own choice of television programme. The eldest of the three women made very little contribution to the discussion until the talk turned to a child who played football in the garden, kicking the ball against the wall of the house for hours on end, then she said, 'I like gardening. I miss having a garden at the hostel. It's not the same when there are lots of other people walking all over it and picking the flowers. We had a nice garden at home. I spent a lot of time out there. It got me out of the way, being in the garden, particularly when Phil was in a bad mood. I like flowers – didn't grow vegetables, perhaps a few tomatoes. Course, this time of year it's a bit bare so I'd pot up some hyacinths for the house. I'd bought a bag of them in the market. Kept some of them back for planting outside. I had a nice blue bowl, the same colour as the flowers, and when they began to grow, pale green shoots coming through, I put them in it and put the bowl on the hall table. They did look lovely.'

She paused to light a cigarette from a green-and-white packet and I could smell the faint scent of menthol. The older woman put the packet and a yellow cigarette lighter on the table, inhaled once and placed the cigarette on the ashtray. She continued to stare out into the lamplit street and her lower lip quivered. Was this woman about to admit to some similar incident? She began slowly and with no trace of emotion.

'He had such a temper and he came in that day in a right one. His tea wasn't strong enough. I'd folded his newspaper the wrong way. It didn't matter what I did, nothing was right.' She raised her voice slightly as if she was reliving the event. 'He was effing and blinding at me and I asked him to stop. He went from the lounge to the kitchen and back again, me following, trying to get him to stop swearing. We were pulling and pushing at each other. You know what it's like?'

The woman moved her chair back so that she was facing the rest of the group. Her voice became stronger and she spoke more emphatically. 'We were in the hall and he pulled away from me, sweeping the flowers onto the floor. The pot broke, there was dirt all over the tiles and the stems of the plants were broken. I was really upset. I do like flowers. I'll give you hyacinths, I thought.'

She stopped and untied the scarf from around her neck, folded it neatly and put it into her pocket, pushed the sleeves of her mac up and continued. 'So a couple of days later I asked him if he fancied a lamb stew.

'"Yes," he said, "That'll be nice."

'I went to the butcher's and bought a bit of neck-end. I made a stew with carrots and peas but instead of onions I used the hyacinth bulbs. I peeled them, chopped them and fried them just as if they were the real thing. I put them with the meat and the other vegetables in a casserole, added some beer to disguise the taste, and cooked it. When he came in from work I gave it to him. He asked me if I was having some. I told him I'd had some earlier. He said he thought it tasted a bit funny. "Mine didn't," I told him. He went on and ate it all up. After about half an hour he started to sweat and said he was going to bed – he didn't feel very well. He was in and out of bed all night going to the toilet and saying he felt sick. The next morning he looked awful. He was all grey and his eyes were dull. He told me to get the doctor. He told the doctor how bad he felt, going to the toilet all the time and feeling nauseous. The doctor said it was food poisoning and asked him what he'd eaten. He'd had a pie a lunchtime in the pub and the lamb stew. He said that the stew had tasted funny. I told the doctor mine hadn't. "It must have been the pie," the doctor said. Anyway, he got a week off work. Kept on about how I'd given him a dodgy stew. I never let on, even after we separated. I've never told anyone.' She paused. 'I do like a nice garden.'

They exchanged glances but before anyone could speak the door of the family court opened, the usher appeared, and Sharon's case was called on. Once in the courtroom I called Sharon to give her account of the incidents that gave rise to the application for an injunction to prevent her boyfriend from contacting her. She wasn't the best of witnesses and I could see that the judge was not impressed. Then cross-examination began with the boyfriend's barrister asking Sharon if she wanted to stay at the hostel or go back to her flat. Sharon hesitated.

'Of course I'd like to go back to the flat.'

The judge interjected. 'Of course she wants to go back to her own home. That Refuge is disgusting.'

'Yes, of course, Your Honour. But I am suggesting that the witness wants to go back to the flat with Mr Fenton.'

'Well, say so.' It was clearly the end of a long day. The judge turned to Sharon and asked her if she did want to go back to her boyfriend.

Sharon looked round the courtroom, first at me with a look of desperation on her face and then at Colin's barrister, who was holding a piece of pale lilac notepaper in his hand. My earlier uneasiness was, I thought, about to be confirmed. Sharon had seen the letter as well and was struggling to find an answer.

'Let me help you,' said Colin's barrister, smiling, and he handed the piece of paper to the usher and asked her to give it to Sharon. Sharon looked at it.

The barrister paused. 'Did you write that?'

'Yes.'

'Would you like to read it to the court?'

Sharon read out the letter she had written asking Colin to meet her at the shop near the Refuge to talk about her going back with their child, Angelina.

'You met Colin by arrangement and went back to the flat with him?'

Sharon's voice was dull. 'Yes.'

'And when you were there, you had intercourse with him.'

'Yes.'

I looked at the judge. He leant forward. 'I don't think you have any grounds for an injunction.' He turned to Sharon and told her to stop being so silly and return home. Then, with a swift nod, he rose and swept off the bench before anyone could get to their feet.

Once outside the courtroom, the three women wanted to know what had happened. Sharon was crying so I told them she had agreed to give Colin another chance for the sake of the child. 'That's right, isn't it?' I said. Sharon nodded her head as she wiped away the tears and blew her nose. They looked at her in amazement, turned on their heels and walked away.

Along the corridor Colin was saying goodbye to his barrister and then he walked up to Sharon and put an arm round her shoulders.

'Come on, let's go and get Angie and your things.' And, without a nod in my direction, the two of them strolled out of the building.

The usher came out of the courtroom and stood watching them for a few moments before turning to me. 'They're such liars, these people, aren't they?'

Unwilling Witnesses

Any system of justice relies on witnesses giving evidence in court, usually live in front of the tribunal of fact be that magistrates or jury. There are many reasons why witnesses fail to attend court, but too often it is because the defendant is the partner. Women are by far the most numerous of these reluctant witnesses.

The police had a reputation of being indifferent to women who made allegations of assault by their partners. These proceedings for assault, frequently referred to as 'domestics', would fail because the victim would refuse to attend court, and that may have been why the police were reluctant to spend time investigating and doing the paperwork for a court hearing When I was a solicitor I would advise women of their rights to take proceedings in the magistrates' court for a separation order and then take divorce proceedings, but very often after a few days I would receive either a letter or a telephone call from the woman saying she didn't want to proceed. Some would say they were too afraid to proceed, others believed it would plunge them into poverty, some didn't like the idea of their children's father going to prison with all its implications.

But the reluctance of women to give evidence against their partners was relied upon by defendants to try and avoid a prison sentence. I had a number of cases like that; two stand out.

Henry was a black male in his late twenties. He was physically strong and worked out in a gym on a regular basis. He also took steroids to enhance his physique. He lived with a slender white woman, Linda, a couple of years younger than himself, who he had known since they were at school together. They had a three-year-old daughter, a beautiful toddler. They appeared to be an ideal family.

However, there were problems lurking beneath the surface. Linda's parents did not approve of their relationship and refused to have Henry in their home. Linda must have found herself pulled in two directions, particularly as they were supportive of her and her child. She would resort to lies when she wanted to go and see her parents and Henry would become violent when he discovered the deception.

Matters came to head on just such an occasion. Linda was ironing some clothes when Henry became suspicious and asked her if she was planning to go to her family. She told him she was and they began to argue.

He said she had to make a choice between her parents and him. She wouldn't agree to that.

After several minutes of verbal abuse on both sides, Henry pushed the ironing board over and grabbed the iron. He then put the hot plate against Linda's cheek. She screamed in anguish at the pain. To make matters worse he refused to get help or let her go to the hospital. When he went to sleep that night she was able to escape and get the burn to her face treated and dressed. Later that night the police arrested Henry and the child was restored to her mother.

Henry was remanded in custody and when I went to see him in Nottingham Jail he insisted Linda wouldn't come to court and give evidence against him. I advised him to be sensible because I believed the antagonism of Linda's parents and the distress their racism caused him was good mitigation. In addition I would have sought expert help on his use of steroids because I knew there was a link between increased aggression and the use of those drugs. He refused.

On the day of the trial, Linda did turn up and I had to go and see Henry in the cells and tell him she was intent on giving evidence against him. He was remarkably calm and agreed to plead guilty. Linda sat through the hearing in tears, a scar the shape of an iron just visible under her make-up.

Henry was sentenced by the trial judge to three years' imprisonment. The prosecution didn't think that was adequate and appealed that decision, and the sentence was increased to six years.

The second case was in some ways more traumatic than the first. My client, Rob, was twenty-two years old and was 'drop-dead gorgeous'. He worked as a gardener in a leafy area of Winchester. A few doors away from one of the gardens where he worked lived Donna, a golden-haired schoolgirl. They began by saying hello to each other but then their conversations became longer.

Rob began to turn up near her home more and more frequently and they began meeting in the evenings. Rob never said if or how far their relationship had progressed and there was no evidence of any illegal sexual relationship. He did tell me he knew she was underage. If there had been such a relationship she wasn't telling either.

Donna's parents became concerned about their daughter's friendship with this older man and demanded she stopped seeing him. She refused to do so at first but eventually she told Rob she could no longer meet him. He seemed to accept it, but then started hanging around her home, hiding in the shrubs and bushes along the street. Donna was frightened by this but refused all his entreaties.

One night when she was on her way out to see a school friend, Rob jumped out from the hedge and grabbed hold of her hand. He demanded she see him again and, when she refused, he pulled her into the garden of the next-door house and hit her across the face. She screamed, calling for her father. Rob produced a knife from his pocket and stabbed her in the arm and leg. A neighbour heard her cries for help and ran to her aid. The police were called and Rob was arrested for assault occasioning grievous bodily harm, more commonly called GBH.

When he came to trial he insisted she would not give evidence against him. Donna had visited him in prison and written letters to him saying she forgave him. When the case was listed for hearing at Winchester Crown Court, she did indeed fail to attend. My application to the judge to dismiss the case was refused and the trial adjourned to another date.

This time she came to the court building. However, when she was called to give evidence she refused to come into the courtroom. The judge who was trying the case asked the jury to leave and had screens erected round the witness box. Donna was told the judge wanted to speak to her in private and she was ushered into the courtroom. Hidden behind screens she could not see Rob; nor could he see her.

The judge then asked her a little about herself and persuaded her that she should tell him about the event. She agreed to do so. The jury were brought back into court and she described the assault. She still had the scars, including a long jagged one on her right arm and another on her shoulder. Before I could start cross-examining her, Rob asked to speak to me. The judge was reluctant to adjourn the case but sent the jury out and let me speak to Rob behind the door to the cells.

Rob asked me what would happen if he conducted the trial himself. I advised him against doing that.

'But will I get to cross-examine her?'

I told him I couldn't guarantee that the screens would be removed. Rob said he would represent himself.

I went back into court and told the judge that Rob had dispensed with my services and would be unrepresented. Despite the judge warning him against taking that course Rob insisted and the trial proceeded without me, but with my solicitor present to advise Rob during the trial.

Rob was convicted and received a sentence of six years' imprisonment. At first he was detained in Winchester Prison and he wrote to Donna asking her to come and see him. I am not aware if she did or not. After a few months he was due to be moved to another prison and he then managed to escape. He was arrested close to Donna's home, returned to prison and some months later committed suicide.

The prosecution aren't too concerned about unwilling witnesses, but calling a witness for the defence who has been arrested and brought to court can be dangerous. Nevertheless, sometimes counsel have to make the decision to do that.

I was representing a man, John, accused of supplying drugs. The evidence against him consisted of a few wraps of cocaine allegedly found in his possession when he was searched at the police station. He had been arrested at his home together with his girlfriend, Emma. The house had been searched and a few items seized. They included scales and small plastic bags. The prosecution said these were the paraphernalia of a drug supplier. Back at the police station John was searched by police officer 'A' who claimed he had found a bag containing five wraps of cocaine concealed in John's clothing.

John claimed the wraps had been planted on him by the officer and the items take from his home were merely ordinary household scales and the plastic bags were of a type anyone might have. There was no forensic evidence of drugs at the property.

Making allegations of this nature against a police officer is usually unsuccessful. But there were chinks in the prosecution evidence. I had asked for disclosure of the intelligence file that had been the reason for John's arrest. At first that was refused but after prosecuting counsel had seen the papers he told the judge there was nothing to prevent me seeing the records. What they showed was that the officer's reason for the arrest was different from that which he had given in his written statement. Further disclosure revealed the officer had already been reprimanded for lying in court in another case. His motive was said to be his desire to be transferred out of uniform to the CID, giving him the status of a detective.

Emma had been present in the police station when the wraps of cocaine were allegedly found in John's pockets. She said she had seen the officer 'A' produce them from a larger plastic bag with blue writing on it – a Metropolitan Police exhibit bag. I sought further disclosure – this time the records of the movement of exhibits bags in the police station. From those records there was evidence officer 'A' had removed a bag of exhibits relating to another case from the exhibits store and then returned it about half an hour later, something he struggled to explain in cross-examination.

Although the trial had gone well from the defence point of view, I wanted to call Emma to give evidence about the drugs being planted. Although she had said she would come to court she didn't do so. Emma was a drug addict and had a conviction for prostitution. I decided to take the risk and asked for the issue of an arrest warrant. That evening she was arrested and held overnight in police cells. In the morning I asked the solicitor's clerk to check she was alright and to confirm she wanted to give evidence. She said she did and with my heart in my mouth I called her into the witness box. Fortunately she was a good witness and corroborated John's account. She withstood cross-examination easily.

'I know what you're trying to get me to say,' she said. 'Before I got hooked on that stuff I read law at university.'

John was acquitted and prosecuting counsel told me he had never enjoyed cross-examining a witness more.

Dolly Parton Lookalike

The two defendants were brother and sister, Charles and Alice Kent. They were charged with an assault occasioning grievous bodily harm on a much older male, Colin. Their mother Rose was divorced from their father and had begun a relationship with Colin. When she told him she no longer wished to see him he became abusive and one night he forced his way into the house and, she alleged, raped her. She reported the rape to the police. They arrested Colin who said Rose had consented. The police, as they often did in those days, advised her it was a waste of time pursuing the allegation.

A few days later, Colin was beaten up by two intruders who broke into his house at night. He said he didn't know his assailants.

There was no apparent motive for the attack save the allegation made by Rose. The police arrested both Charles and Alice. During their interviews with the police they both denied being the person or persons who had committed the assault. The police held an identification parade although Colin had met both Charles and Alice previously. Not surprisingly, he picked them out on the parade. The police charged the brother and sister with the offence.

At trial they both pleaded not guilty, saying they had been at home at the time of the offence: the defence of alibi. They were not calling any witnesses to support their claim. I was representing Charles and another female barrister was defending Alice.

The prosecution case was flawed by the prosecution witness's failure to identify the brother and sister at the time of the attack.

Where cases are based on an identification made after the event, the prosecution have to serve on the defence the first description given by the witnesses. This is usually the notes of a police officer who attends the scene of the crime. It is not part of the prosecution case, but it is often a rich source of material for defending counsel. So it was in this case. Colin had described the two people who had assaulted him as being white males of similar height, both wearing dark clothing. The description could have been my client (and many others) but it did not fit the description of his sister. She was female, she was about six inches shorter than her brother, and she had a figure like Dolly Parton. Not exactly a second male.

The jury didn't take long to acquit Alice, but they failed to agree on my client. In most cases the prosecution would ask for a retrial, but the acquittal of Alice called into question the whole identification process and they decided not to do so. Alice's barrister thought they had got away with it. She may have been right, but if they had there was a certain element of rough justice in the outcome.

Another Silly Judge

I have already written about judges and their idiosyncrasies, and a further example concerned the trial for theft by a young woman, Shelley. She was alleged to have stolen clothes from a shop in Chelmsford, a charge she denied. By the time the case came to trial she was six months pregnant. It was not an easy pregnancy and I attended court with a doctor's report saying that if she wanted to give birth to the child she was to have complete rest.

I applied to the judge to have the case adjourned until after the baby was born. He agreed to that request if my solicitors would give an undertaking to advise the court when Shelley was fit to attend. The case would then be listed for hearing.

Every court has a list officer who is responsible for ensuring that all the courtrooms have sufficient work for the day and that cases are heard as quickly as possible. Some are better than others. Counsels' clerks check the lists every night and allocate barristers to cover each and every case. As far as possible the advocate will be the one chosen by the solicitor.

About three months after the initial listing of Shelley's case I was told by my clerk that her case was to be heard the next day. That evening the solicitors phoned me at home to say not only had they not contacted the list office, but Shelley had not yet had her baby.

At court the next day I found the case had been listed as a floater which meant there was no court immediately available to hear it. I went to see the list officer, a rather grumpy woman, and asked her why it had been listed when Shelley's solicitors had not spoken to her office. She insisted they had told her the baby had been born. I repeated that Shelley had not given birth and, rather than keep witnesses, lawyers and police officers waiting she should release us. She refused and said the case should be called and the judge make the decision.

When it was called into court the list officer insisted she had been told that the case could be heard. I requested another adjournment; Shelley was at her due date and was likely to go into labour at any moment.

'Your client is pregnant, not ill, and I can't see any reason why this trial should not go ahead today,' the judge said.

I tried again to persuade him it would not be wise to have Shelley brought to court.

'No, Miss Barnes. This case is very old and should be heard now. All the witnesses are here. Once your client is at court we'll begin.'

'I see Your Honour is skilled in obstetrics?'

I shouldn't have said that, but couldn't resist. He stormed off the bench and suddenly we were told there was no court time that day.

One is a Tragedy, Three is Murder

Daphne Williams was a sorry sight: a crumpled grey cardigan, a non-too-clean dress and pink fluffy slippers. I had gone to see her at the secure hospital to which she had been remanded after being charged with the murder of her three children.

The first of her children had died when he was about fifteen months old and an autopsy had given the cause of death as sudden infant death syndrome, SIDs, more commonly called a cot death, and an underlying viral infection. Her second child, also a son, died at eight months and again the cause of death was SIDS. The third infant was about seven months old when he was found struggling for breath and very floppy in a swing chair attached to a door frame. Again there was no obvious cause of death and the pathologist signed a death certificate citing SIDS.

When Daphne became pregnant with a fourth child Social Services stepped in and began proceedings to take the child away at birth. At a joint meeting between social workers and police liaison officers, they discussed Daphne's case and how to present the case for removing the baby from Daphne's care. The police officer suggested Daphne should see Professor Sir Roy Meadows, who was a paediatrician at the Children's Hospital in Leeds. He had become concerned by the number of children presenting with injuries for which there was no satisfactory explanation. This included babies dying without any clear medical diagnosis. He came to believe the children were being assaulted by their parents and in some of the cases he suggested the parent had a psychiatric condition which he named Munchausen's syndrome by proxy. Munchausen's is a well-known, if rare mental health condition, which manifests itself in the patient presenting with medical conditions they do not have. They are often so persuasive that doctors treat them for the illness. Munchausen's by proxy differs in that the parent alleges his/her child has a problem, and seeks medical intervention. Meadows went further and, when any children died without what he considered a proper reason for the death, he claimed 'One child's death is a tragedy, two is suspicious, three is murder.'

At the instigation of Social Services, Daphne agreed to go and see him. On the train going north from London with a social worker and a police officer (quite why the police were there was never explained), Daphne suddenly confessed to killing all three children. She was immediately taken back to the police station in East London and interviewed under caution in the presence of a solicitor, and again said she had killed all three children.

The case against her relied in its entirety on her confessions and Professor Meadows' assertion that she had killed them by suffocation – probably a pillow pressed against their faces. He claimed she suffered from Munchausen's by proxy, although he never met her, nor did he examine her history or that of her children.

Daphne was not an easy client; one minute she would say she had killed her children and then say she hadn't. The psychologists at the hospital who had the opportunity to assess her mental health said she was prone to confabulate – she couldn't distinguish between her lies and the truth. Not one, though, suggested she had Munchausen's.

We were able to argue that her confessions were unreliable and should not be admitted in evidence. The prosecution psychologist had come to the same conclusion and the case against her was dismissed.

Had she killed her children? Care proceedings in the High Court did find on a balance of probabilities that she had. I wasn't involved in those proceedings but as it happened a former pupil of mine was, representing the local authority. She told me they had relied on Professor Meadows' evidence, whose methods have now been discredited.

Removing her fourth child from her care was probably the right decision, but Daphne's real offence was being poor and educationally challenged. All three children were born premature and were probably liable to have problems. The advice about preventing cot deaths would have involved her remembering to lay the baby on its back. She probably couldn't remember that. They may not have been able to afford to buy new mattresses for the cot. In addition, both Daphne and her husband were heavy smokers – not ideal with a young child. They would have struggled with caring for any child without help, help that was not available.

A Humongous Box of Cannabis

Ellie was a divorced woman in her late forties charged with importing a large quantity of cannabis. The whole case reminded me of a Keystone Cops film. It had started with the police being informed that a warehouse on the eastern outskirts of London was being used for the storage of drugs after they had been imported into the country. The packages were in wooden containers and were collected from there to be distributed and sold. The police kept observation on the premises after a consignment of cannabis had been identified using sniffer dogs.

Ellie, her current boyfriend and another man turned up with the paperwork to collect this consignment in a white van. There were three large boxes and they were too big to fit into the vehicle. After trying to get all three in, Ellie said they would leave one and come back for it. The foreman was reluctant for them to do that. I suspected he was the police informant and knew the contents of the boxes. However, they couldn't get all three into the van and in the end they set off with just two.

They drove through East London followed at a distance by an unmarked police car. The police lost them as they tried to navigate a route into the City. Ellie and her companions eventually stopped at an empty property that was being renovated, where they attempted to unload the boxes. They had nothing to help them do so.

As they debated what to do, the police caught up with them and the subsequent events were recorded on a video. They must have decided to break into the boxes because the film showed one of the two men go into the property and come out with a crowbar. They began to lever open the first of the two boxes. As they began to break it open, the wooden crate toppled out of the van and fell, breaking into pieces and spilling its contents onto the road.

'There was this humongous pile of brown slabs,' Ellie said.

At that point the police decided to intervene. Ellie and the two men were standing open-mouthed at the contents of the box. The video showed broken pieces of wood and packages, about the size of a large bag of flour, strewn all over the road and pavement. The police rushed towards Ellie and her two companions, grabbed them and placed then under arrest. 'Caught bang to rights,' one might say.

In interview Ellie gave a full account of how she came to be involved in this importation. It would have been unbelievable in a novel. She told the police that she had been contacted by a man who asked her to meet him in Wardour Street to talk about a film he was producing. The mention of Wardour Street confirmed for her that he was a film producer. She went to the address he gave her and he met her at the door of some offices. He said they needed to talk in a café as his colleague was having a meeting in the office.

The man then told her he wanted someone to do a fake run of some items from a warehouse in Essex into Central London. Her job would be to look for landmarks suitable for a film and to time the journey. She believed him because, she said, she had done similar work in the past. She told me she had run one of the stages at Glastonbury and assumed he had got her name from one her previous employers. When she asked where the items would be delivered, he told her that didn't matter. When she had found somewhere she should let him know and he would arrange for them to be picked up. He told her the items were in quite large boxes and she would need to hire a van. When she agreed to do it he gave her a lading note for three items and enough money to hire a van.

She realised she would need help, so she recruited her boyfriend Harold and his friend Peter. It was Peter who suggested the building site as somewhere to take the boxes. He was employed by the construction company at the site and knew that there was no work taking place for a few weeks. Harold hired the van and off they went to the warehouse.

Ellie was expecting to collect three cardboard boxes and was surprised to discover the three wooden crates. She was equally surprised by their weight. They struggled getting them into the van and there wasn't sufficient space for all three. She agreed with the evidence of the foreman. There had been an argument about them leaving one of the boxes behind. There was no dispute about the evidence of the police who followed them and arrested them.

Her two co-defendants told the police that Ellie had asked for their help and they had no knowledge of the contents of the crates. They did say there had been an argument between Ellie and Harold on the way back about the contents. Ellie had told them there was nothing to worry about.

An unbelievable story, but when the unused material was disclosed it was clear that the police had been investigating a number of other people. As I had guessed, the foreman at the warehouse was a police informant. He was he who had told them of the suspect consignments – there had been others.

The Dutch company who had shipped the crates Ellie collected had sent similar consignments to the same warehouse. The staff there all described the boxes being collected by men and not women.

I and the barristers representing Harold and Peter asked for more information about these other shipments. The prosecution then revealed another man, who told a similar story to the one Ellie described, had been prosecuted. He had been approached by a man in a pub and after they had been talking for a while he was offered a job, moving some boxes from the same warehouse in Essex to Central London. In his case the man had told him to bring the van to a street close to the public house and leave the rear unlocked. He was to return the vehicle to the hirers the next day. When this man's case had come to court his lawyers argued for disclosure of the identity of the informant. The prosecution did not want to reveal that, claiming public interest immunity. The procedure for such an application is for the judge to hear the evidence in private and then decide whether the evidence should be kept a secret as being in the public interest or whether the defendant's right to a fair trial is prejudiced. The judge having seen the evidence said it should be given to the defence. When the prosecution declined to do so the only option open to them was not to proceed with the prosecution and the man was formally found not guilty

The man was called to give evidence in Ellie's trial by one of the co-defending counsel. Prosecuting counsel was in some difficulty because the police case was that the man was guilty of the offence and the not guilty verdict was because of a technical issue, but counsel couldn't go behind the verdict.

The jury were out considering Ellie's case for a long time. They acquitted the two men but couldn't agree on Ellie's guilt. The prosecution had chosen to charge them with a conspiracy to import drugs rather than a charge of possession with intent to supply and in order to establish a conspiracy there must be at least one other co-conspirator. As the two men had been acquitted and the words 'and others unknown' had not been in the indictment, Ellie was acquitted as well.

Death of a Designer

Ozzie Clark was a well-known fashion designer in the nineteen sixties. He and his wife, Celia Birtwell, were responsible for some of the most iconic clothes of the period; flowery prints on flowing dresses. Their portrait painted by David Hockney is in the National Gallery, the pair, sitting on opposite sides of a window together with their cat Percy, seem the epitome of the age of Aquarius.

Ozzie's life did not end in such grace. His star faded after he and Celia separated and then divorced. By the time he died he was living in a council flat in North Kensington with his lover, an Italian called Diego Franelli. Diego suffered from mental health issues and Ozzie suggested he seek advice from the psychiatrist who had treated him. Diego did and was given a prescription for the drug Prozac.

What Diego did not know was that Prozac reacted adversely with certain other drugs, particularly the illegal ones he was taking. The effect of this combination of drugs was to make Diego psychotic and in this state he came to believe that Ozzie was the devil and that he must kill him. He picked up a large flowerpot and began to hit Ozzie about the head. He went on beating his lover until he was dead and then ran from the flat.

Some hours later he had reached the outskirts of Richmond Park. From there he rang the police and confessed to killing Ozzie Clark. The police visited the flat to check Ozzie was indeed dead. Other officers made for the park. The gates of the park were locked and they had to scale the walls to enter it. It was a clear moonlit night, which aided their search for Diego. When they found him he was howling like a dog at the moon.

When I received the brief to represent Franelli, I was horrified by the photographs of the scene in the council flat. The walls, which were hung with luscious fabrics, were spattered with blood and brains. The lifeless body of Ozzie Clark was slumped across the deep purple comforter on the bed.

Diego was not fit to be interviewed immediately after his arrest because of his mental state so he was remanded to a secure hospital. Doctors examining him there took blood samples and found traces of Prozac and the illegal amphetamines Diego was taking; their opinion was that at the time of the killing he was suffering from a mental illness.

The diagnosis provided Diego a defence to the charge of murder and he pleaded guilty to the offence of manslaughter. Had the Prozac not been prescribed by a doctor that defence would not have been available as the courts hold a defendant responsible for actions taken when under the influence of alcohol or drugs, because the mental state is then self-induced. Diego pleaded guilty to the offence of manslaughter and this plea was accepted by the prosecution, their own experts having come to the same conclusion as to his mental state. A conviction for murder would have left Diego facing a sentence of life imprisonment; instead he was sentenced to six years' imprisonment.

The Stolen Baby

For six weeks the nation stood on tenterhooks as newspapers, radio and television reported on the search for a day-old baby taken from St Thomas's Hospital in Central London. The breakthrough came when an assistant in a chemist's shop in Buckinghamshire served a woman with nappies and baby food. The shop assistant recognised the woman as one who had recently moved into a cottage in the village. Apart from that she knew nothing about the woman but was surprised by the purchase as she hadn't noticed the woman was pregnant. She decided to call the police.

When the police went to the cottage they found the baby Hannah well and in good health. The woman, Jane Hancock, was arrested and interviewed. She admitted taking the baby but broke down and cried uncontrollably and the interview with her was terminated. The police called a doctor, who advised she be transferred to hospital. She was admitted to a secure hospital where she was diagnosed with Munchausen's syndrome.

Jane's story was a very sad one. At the age of sixteen she had gone home from school to find her father having a heart attack. Apart from calling for an ambulance she didn't know what to do to help him and when he died she felt guilty. She decided to train as a nurse and qualified some five years later. During her training she met and married a soldier and they had two children before he was posted to Northern Ireland. Jane and the two children went with him and it was there that she gave birth to her third child, Kirsty.

Kirsty was born with a hole in her heart and needed immediate surgery. She was to stay in hospital in intensive care for many months and required further operations. Jane's husband became very distressed and there came a point where he was reluctant to agree to any more interventions.

'It was difficult,' Jane told me, 'you've got this child but you can't hold her, cuddle her, touch her. She was so frail.'

After Kirsty came out of hospital the family were relocated to England, but their marriage couldn't be saved. Jane separated from her husband and they began divorce proceeding. Their three children remained living with their father. I could never find out why, because it's unusual for fathers to be given custody of such young children, although it may have been because he could provide them with a home and she could not.

Jane took a job in a nursing home and began a relationship with the owner. He was married but his wife lived on the Isle of

Wight and he spend most of his time living in one of the nursing homes he owned. Jane believed he would marry her, but he wouldn't leave his wife. In an effort to persuade him to do so Jane told him she was pregnant. He seemed to believe her despite her having told him she had had a partial hysterectomy. However, he still wouldn't agree to divorce his wife. When the time came for a baby to arrive Jane decided to steal a child.

She knew St Thomas's because she had had a kidney removed there. She went to the hospital and picked on Hannah's mother because they shared a surname. Jane told her she needed to take the baby away to be weighed. Then she walked out of the hospital, took the train to Amersham and walked to the rented cottage. She had enough baby food, nappies and toiletries for a few weeks; it was when she needed more that she made the mistake of going to the small pharmacy where the shop assistant became suspicious.

Jane must have been suffering from Munchausen's for some time. She had presented to various doctors with symptoms which resulted in an operation to remove a kidney. There was nothing wrong with her kidneys. The same thing had happened with the partial hysterectomy – a second operation that was not needed. She was so persuasive because of her medical training and her extensive contact with hospitals and the medical profession.

Several months had passed by the time the case was heard and she pleaded guilty to the offence of abduction. Because of her mental ill health she was committed to a secure hospital for further treatment. She was released a few months later. Such was the interest, the courtroom was packed with journalists and TV reporters and it was reported on the front page of every newspaper.

Usually, at the end of a case, the barrister gives the brief back to his instructing solicitor, prepares the bill and moves on to the next trial. One has no knowledge of the fate of either the defendant or the victims. But I do know what happened to Jane, Hannah and her mother. I received a telephone call about three years after the trial from a journalist, who told me Jane had died of cancer.

I learnt of Hannah and her mother when Hannah was eighteen. I was reading *The Times* on the day the A-level results came out and on the front cover was a photograph of a mother and daughter. The article in the newspaper identified them as Hannah and her mother. The mother had told the reporter she had found it difficult to bond with Hannah after that initial separation. She had saved the money she was paid for a number of interviews to pay for Hannah to go to private school. Hannah had just passed her exams with four grade A-starred and was going to Manchester University to study mathematics. At least something positive came out of the difficult start the mother and child had.

Other Books by Margaret Barnes

I published my first novel in 2014. It is called *Crucial Evidence* and it begins where most crime novels finish – with the arrest of the offender. But have they arrested the right person? *Crucial Evidence* follows the trial of a young man accused of murder through the trial process. The reviews on Amazon gave it 4 or 5 stars.

It has been described as being '... *both emotionally and intellectually stretching. The economy of the writing still allows empathy with the characters, and the insight into law practice in Britain leads to some uncomfortable recognition.*'

And '*A very believable and compulsive account of the trial and an insight into the inner workings at The Old Bailey in the pursuit of Justice.'*

And finally *'The author draws on her experience in the practice of law to create a realistically vivid portrayal of London's legal system. The intricate detail of the various actors and roles provides a necessary solid (factual) foundation for the fictional account with the real-time, verbatim court proceedings stations the reader in the gallery of this tensely mesmerising drama.'*

In my second novel, *Reluctant Consent,* Barrister Cassie Hardman is being stalked by an unknown male. She doesn't know why but there is some connection to the defendant Paul Sadler, who faced trial for rape.

Cassie struggles with the unwanted invasion into her life as she works on a murder trial – her most important case to date. Each communication forces her to relive her role in the Sadler trial. Again, the workings of the criminal justice system are in the spotlight, in particular the role of a woman like Cassie defending a man accused of rape.

If you have enjoyed reading this book of memoir I would be delighted if you would leave a review.

If you would like to contact me, my email address is *contact@scribblingadvocate.com*